On the preceding pages
in order of appearance:

North Vietnamese
prisoners captured in the
course of Operations
Hickory and Lam Son
54, May 24, 1967.

A scene on the
Antonine column in
Rome depicting the
decapitation of German
prisoners captured in
battle by the Romans,
circa 55 BC.

American parachutists
downed in the fierce
aeriel combat which
accompanied the D-Day
invasion. This picture
from an unidentified
camp was taken on June
14, 1944.

An Argentine taken
prisoner in the
Falklands War, 1983.

MAJOR PAT REID MBE MC
AND MAURICE MICHAEL

PRISONER
OF WAR

Personalkarte I: Personelle Angaben   Oflag VIII F

Kriegsgefangenen-Stammlager:

Lager: Oflag VIII F   Nr. 1519

Name: TOWLE.

Vorname: FREDERIC HARRY DERBY.

Geburtstag und -ort: 12/5/10

Religion: CHURCH ENG.

Vorname des Vaters: FREDERICK.

Familienname der Mutter: HURST.

Staatsangehörigkeit: BRITISH.

Dienstgrad: HPTM.

Truppenteil: ARMY.   Komp. usw.:

Zivilberuf: OHNE.   Berufs-Gr.: 91909

Matrikel Nr. (Stammrolle des Heimatstaates): 28/6/42 AFRIKA.

Gefangennahme (Ort und Datum): GESUND.

Ob gesund, krank, verwundet eingeliefert:

Größe: 180   Haarfarbe: BRAUN

WIFE:- MRS. F.H. TOWLE, 79, HOLMELACY ROAD, HEREFORD, ENGLAND.

Beaufort Books
Publishers
New York

Library of Congress Cataloging-in-
Publication Data

Reid, P.R. (Patrick Robert), 1910–
    Prisoner of war

    Bibliography: p.
    Includes index.
    1. Prisoners of war—History.
    I. Michael, Maurice, 1909–
    II. Title.
    D25.5.R43 1986   355.1′26   85–28751
    ISBN 0–8253–0372–9

Published in the United States by Beaufort
Books Publishers, New York.

Designer: Roger Hammond

Printed in Great Britain
First American Edition

10 9 8 7 6 5 4 3 2 1

C O N T E N T S

Acknowledgements

The authors gratefully acknowledge their debt to the staffs of the British Library, Deutsche Historische Institut, Henfield Public Library, Imperial War Museum, London Library, National Archive and Record Service, Washington, D.C. Public Records Office, Royal Military Academy, Central Library, for their expert and kindly assistance; to Mr John Brason for providing the facts concerning the execution of two German naval deserters in Amsterdam in May 1945, to Lieut Colonel J M B Isaac for many helpful suggestions, to Conte Alain d'Estutt d'Assy for introducing them to the work of Jean Morin, as well as to Mr Ian Scott and the many other authors of books and war diaries, published and unpublished, for permission to quote extracts; but, above all, to the late Frederick Towle, who did much of the early research.

INTRODUCTION

The prisoner of war, not a criminal, not a transgressor, merely an unfortunate who has been defeated in an armed struggle, has nearly always been unwanted, the most unwanted person on earth. In the old days, if he were rich enough to buy his own freedom, that he was allowed to do; if he were physically fit and strong he might be kept as slave labour, for a slave is what he became, but otherwise, beyond the fact that the captor had to deny his enemy the services of his captives what to do with them was a real problem.

This book describes how this problem has been solved down the ages, the fate of the prisoner of war, what he has suffered and the conditions he has had to endure. These latter vary in the extreme; in fact there is no story of appalling suffering or civilized treatment that some ex-POW cannot cap.

The great determinant in the treatment of the POW has always been numbers. Small numbers are easy to deal with in a humane and civilized manner, while logistical difficulties make it impossible to deal with large numbers in anything approaching a humane manner, let alone as prescribed by the various conventions that now provide the international rules for their treatment. In the days of cannon fodder many of the rank and file were 'disposable', but today when it takes months or years to train a fighter pilot, a tank crew or the crew of a complex piece of artillery, no member of the armed forces can be spared; hence the imperative need for those captured to try to escape and rejoin their armies. Indeed, it is becoming questionable whether in the next war either side can afford to take prisoners, supposing they ever get close enough to each other to do so. Perhaps the only surrender acceptable will be that of the whole country involved; otherwise no quarter will be given.

CHAPTER   I

PRISONER
OF WAR

The live prisoner provided his captor with slave labour; the head (of the unwanted captive) was evidence of his prowess.

'As soon as your enemy has laid down his arms and surrendered his body, you no longer have any right over his life'. That was the revolutionary view formulated by the French humanitarian law maker Vattel in 1758 which came to be generally accepted in the West, so that the soldier who surrendered to the enemy could confidently expect that he would be treated with humanity. This has not always been the case.

In primitive warfare, it was probably your head, scalp or testicles the enemy sought and which he wanted in order to demonstrate his prowess or enhance his virility; but he certainly did not want *you*. Later, wars were often waged to obtain people to colonize new land, as was the case with the Assyrians, when Tiglath-Pilaser and then Sennacherib captured and removed the tribes of Reuben and Gad and the people of Samaria to lands beyond the Euphrates, but the enemy warrior as such was only wanted for himself once the institution of slavery had been invented.

The institution of slavery gave human life a value it had not previously had, making healthy men and women a source of wealth. In those early days war was total in that if a territory was conquered or a city taken, whatever was in it belonged to the victor: men, women and children, their goods and property — it was all his to do what he liked with. Able-bodied men and women captured in war could be taken home as the captor's own slaves or be sold to others as their slaves. It was only when there was no accessible market or means of getting your human merchandise to it and the enemy had captured none of your own men for whom you could have exchanged his, that you slaughtered your captives.

It is true that some early religions required a number of captives for ritual slaughter in the victory celebrations. This was the lot of some of the Roman legionaries captured by the Teutons when they decisively defeated

Varus in AD 9 — they were burned alive in front of the Teutons' altars. The Assyrians, Egyptians and Romans all displayed numbers of captives in their victory parades or triumphs, as King Henry did after Agincourt (1415), as Hitler planned to do, and as the Soviets actually did in Moscow on July 17, 1944 when they paraded 37 000 bedraggled German prisoners to the populace. After being thus displayed, the more eminent captives, like Vercingetorix, the Gallic commander taken at the successful siege of Alesia, would be killed. Vercingetorix was publicly strangled, and the others were sold off as slaves or sent to the galleys. The Romans also employed considerable numbers of their younger and stronger captives as gladiators, first sending them to the gladiatorial schools, where they were trained for public combat in the arena. That at least granted them a respite of a few more months, even years of life. The janissaries of later centuries were mostly youths of good physique, similarly captured and specially trained.

RANSOMING

As those captured in war were *ipso facto* your property and could be sold into slavery, it was logical that some might be persuaded to buy themselves. People of substance might be induced to pay considerable sums for their release and freedom: a ransom. It is not known when this practice first started, but the oldest available set of laws, the Code of Hammurabi the Assyrian, makes various rules governing the paying of ransoms, so that the system must have been established by 2000 BC, if not long before.

The Assyrian soldier gave his services in return for land and thus was a man of substance, and it was laid down that he should be responsible for his own ransom. This might in the first instance be paid by an intermediary, acting as a sort of pawnbroker, who advanced the money, which was later repaid with interest added. If the ransomed soldier could not raise enough to pay what was due, the temple at which he worshipped was supposed to assist and, failing that, the landowner from whom the soldier had his land. Under no circumstances was the soldier's house or orchard to be sold to pay the ransom, so the payment of a ransom never utterly ruined an Assyrian as it did many a medieval knight. With the Greeks and Romans ransoms were again sometimes paid by an intermediary, when the person concerned became the property of the intermediary, who could enjoy his services until such times as his family could repay the sum advanced.

The unwanted or surplus captive was treated with a callous cruelty that to us is horrifying (though contemporaries evidently did not find it so), cruelty that today seems gratuitous, unmotivated. The translation of one cuneiform tablet reads: 'I captured people alive and impaled them on stakes before the city'. Another: 'I have captured many men alive; with some I have had their hands or arms cut off, with others their nose or ears; I have put out the eyes of many — torn out the tongues of others — cut off their lips'. A history of the Punic Wars describes how the Carthaginians captured the Roman general Spendius, and then crucified him and several others in full view of the Roman camp. Then the Carthaginian general responsible carelessly let himself be captured by the Romans, who

> 'at once took him to the cross on which Spendius was hanging, and after the infliction of exquisite tortures, took down the latter's body and fastened Hannibal, still living, to this cross; and then slaughtered thirty Carthaginians of the highest rank round the corpse of Spendius.'

Before this, in 352 BC, when Alexander the Great at Krokos defeated the Phokians, themselves reputed to have made their captives jump off a high

The Soviet version of the Roman triumph: German prisoners being paraded through the streets of Leningrad to encourage the belief that the Russians were winning. Hitler hoped to be able to stage the same sort of spectacle and threatened to include Major Reid in the parade, but Fate decreed otherwise.

cliff to their death, and found that he had captured 3000 men he did not want, he drowned them all. (Two thousand years later the Soviets used the same expedient to rid themselves of 7000 unwanted Polish officers they held as prisoners of war, putting them into barges which they towed out into the White Sea and abandoned there with the seacocks open.)

Could prisoners in classical times who were not ransomed have expected any other fate than death? It was important in that type of warfare to deprive the enemy of his effective power and so avoid another attack; thus, though your main enemy's allies, who were only fighting you because they were bound by treaty to do so, might be allowed to go home, the real enemy had to be rendered harmless and some did this by killing, others in another way. For example, after one naval battle the Athenians cut off the right hand of each of the enemy rowers they captured, thus depriving the opposing fleet of its crews without actually killing them. Mutilation was also practised by the Chinese, for it is recorded that King Wau, a 'just king' who reigned in BC China, although he had the commanders of captured forces put to death, released the rank and file after each had had one ear sliced off. For this he was considered 'humane'. One Greek emperor is said to have blinded 15 000 Bulgarians (1500 is the more likely figure) before sending them home. The most civilized of the ancients, however, appear to have been the Indians, whose laws forbade the killing of any enemy who asked for quarter or surrendered. (Nor was it allowed to kill an enemy when he was asleep, weaponless or otherwise unable to defend himself. You were not even supposed to attack a man who was already engaged in combat with one of your own side.)

As warfare developed and became more a matter of besieging towns and cities, the ancient world did follow a set of tacitly accepted conventions. Soldiers in a beleaguered city that surrendered were not killed, but allowed to march out with a minimum of clothing and a meagre, though adequate amount of food.

'I captured people alive and impaled them on stakes before the city' records a cuneiform tablet, and the same fate befell one of these prisoners. Note the unusual way in which the hands are tied.

If the besieged city had employed mercenaries and the mercenaries were compatriots of the victor, they were regarded as traitors and for treachery the penalty was death (as it was two thousand years later for those Ukrainians, Byelorussians, and Cossacks who, while Soviet citizens though not Russian nationals, had donned German uniform in the vain hope of winning their freedom). Otherwise, the untainted mercenary was often recruited into the victor's own army. The Persians and Eygptians branded mercenaries with an identification mark. Not all commanders wanted mercenaries. Some considered them expensive, because they had to be paid, and so tended not to employ them, while others — Jagietto of Lithuania for one — held that if you were victorious the booty you took would more than pay for the mercenaries, while if you were defeated one and all would be killed or taken prisoner, and in either event the mercenaries would be unable to present a bill. On the other hand, there is at least one instance of a victor paying the mercenaries he recruited from the enemy the back pay owed to them by the city that had surrendered.

The only improvement in a prisoner's lot came with the revival of the system of ransoming, which gave those of some substance a chance of redeeming life and liberty. Even then, they were mostly lumped in with the rest of the booty to which the ransom money was added. Those without means to buy themselves were either hanged to be rid of them, or left to fend for themselves. In a strange country with no one to help them, if they were to live, they had to steal or take by force what they could, when they could, and as a result every man's hand was against them. When the numbers involved were great, the release of prisoners caused a serious problem, as after the Battle of Pavia in 1525 when 20 000 Frenchmen, who were judged unable to pay a ransom, were freed. They roamed about in small bands pillaging and looting — and starving. In the end they had to be rounded up and escorted to the frontier, the worst offenders being killed in the process. There was, however, no food to give them on the way and the roads to the frontier were left lined with corpses. One of the survivors Blaise de Montluc recorded that during his march of more than 186 miles he ate only turnip and cabbage.

The mounted knight was in a very different position; indeed, he was often a source of considerable profit. His horse and armour went to his captor, his person and the ransom for it, less a small proportion for the captor, went to the army commander, or, in the case of a king, to the captor's king.

THE PRICE OF A PRISONER'S LIFE

In classical times the average price of a prisoner was 80–100 drachmae (about £20), a person of eminence obviously fetching considerably more. The price of human life continued to rise. Jan Dtugosz a Polish chronicler records that in 1122 a Bohemian prince, who had made a great nuisance of himself by his repeated raids into Polish territory, was finally captured and taken to Cracow where he was imprisoned. The Poles demanded a ransom of 80 000 marks in silver and after considerable haggling agreement was reached on 20 000 marks (say £15 000), of which 12 000 marks were to be paid in cash before the prince was released, the prince providing his own son as hostage for payment of the balance, which, when it arrived, was in the form of 50 silver vessels, mostly goblets and drinking vessels of 'Greek workmanship'. At the other end of the scale, a mere 1500 marks was paid by one Kuno of Stadt Barberg. The standard rate, however, seems to have been one year's gross income, so that the real point at issue was what the prisoner's true income was.

When kings were captured, as happened to Richard Coeur de Lion, King John of France and King David of Scotland, the sums required were so enormous that they could only be found by raising extra taxation, even though under the feudal system all tenants or vassals of a lord were obliged to contribute towards his ransom if he became a prisoner of war. King John cost his country 6000 livres, the sum paid by the Duke of Bedford to Count de Ligny for Joan of Arc.

SPECTACULAR RANSOMS

Alongside this ransoming of prisoners there developed a parallel system of barter, of exchange of knight for knight, and so on, as had been practised a thousand years earlier. The emphasis was always on the payment of a ransom; indeed, there was so much money in ransoming that civilian speculators used to arrive on the battlefield and buy up prisoners from their captors. In the reign of Edward III (1312–77), Sir Walter Manny is said to have made the enormous sum of £8000 — equivalent perhaps to a million today. Not even the king was above lining his pocket in this way, for it is recorded that after the Battle of Agincourt, the king of England and the lords of his suite bought from the 'lower soldiery' all 'prisoners of consideration'.

Payment was not automatic. Jean de Rodemark was a member of one of the foremost families of Luxembourg. He and his wife were seigneurs of at least seven estates, which at the start of the fifteenth century were said to have produced an income of 14–15 000 florins, while Jean's personal estate was estimated at 50 000 florins — in other words, he was a rich man. He certainly considered himself such when he and his son went to war in 1431 on behalf of René of Anjou with a half promise that the king would see them right if the worst came to the worst and either had to produce a ransom. In the event both were captured by the Burgundians at Bulgoneville that July, the son ending up in the hands of Antoine de Croy and Jean himself in those of Antoine de Toulonjon.

Jean de Rodemark's ransom was finally fixed at 18 000 'florins d'or du Rhin', which was thought to correspond to one year's income. In those days the debtor's word was no longer enough and guarantees had to be found before the person being ransomed could go free. Having finally succeeded in obtaining the necessary guarantees, Jean set out to collect the money. René de Anjou honoured his promise as far as Jean's son was concerned, but he could only help Jean himself with a rather vague promise of 10 000 florins to be paid in several instalments. In fact he paid 6000 florins to one of Jean's guarantors a year later but that was all. Jean sold what he could and so raised 8000 florins, but this left him owing 4000 florins plus 714 for expenses incurred. In times of war with bands of armed men roaming the countryside, the farmers may well have found it difficult to pay their dues and without the expected income from his lands, Jean found himself in dire straits.

Then his captor Antoine de Toulonjon died and the debt passed to the latter's son, Jean. One of de Rodemark's guarantors also died and Jean's obligation to him devolved on his son, also Jean. As this Jean seemed unable to pay, Jean de Toulonjon started suing the third guarantor for the outstanding 4714 florins. There then followed 33 years of stalling and evasive manoeuvring involving the courts in Dijon and elsewhere and even Parliament, with creditors at various times threatening to make use of their right, though an archaic one, to dishonour de Rodemark. This involved hanging an effigy of the person being dishonoured by the feet from a gallows and at the same time posting placards proclaiming the creditor's loss of honour on the gates of his châteaux and throughout his lands. This extreme measure had been used in the past mainly in time of war, when recourse to the civil courts was difficult or impossible. In the end Jean de Rodemark was forced to dispose of all or almost all his estates and, in 1465, the last of the ransom was paid, the final payment being made to someone who had bought the debt from the son of the original captor.

Sometimes the ransom demanded was so huge that the captive could not raise the money and died in prison with the amount unpaid. Others took years to collect the sum required. The Duke of Orleans, taken prisoner at Agincourt, did not regain his freedom for 25 years, spent mostly in Windsor Castle, Pomfret Castle and the Tower.

Obviously, anyone who sported especially magnificent armour or rich caparison was advertising himself as a profitable person to capture.

On the other hand, failure to advertise your true status could be fatal. The number of Scots gentlemen killed during the battle of Musselburgh outside Edinburgh in 1548 would not have been anything like as great as it was, Patin — that clergyman-Jacobite turned 'supergrass' — tells us, if they had dressed as gentlemen. 'Their mean appearance gave little hope of their ability to pay ransom' and so they were killed instead of being taken prisoner. 'As for woordes and goodly proffer of great ranndsomes wear as common and ryfe in the mouths of the tone as in toother'; but as they were all clad alike and there was 'not one with either cheyne, brooch, ryng or garment of silke that I could see . . .', so that there was no knowing which, if any, would be good for a ransom.

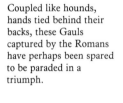
Coupled like hounds, hands tied behind their backs, these Gauls captured by the Romans have perhaps been spared to be paraded in a triumph.

KNIGHTS AS PRISONERS

A knight was not always taken prisoner by another knight. Unhorsed and, if in full armour, probably unable to rise because of its weight, a recumbent knight could well be captured by a common soldier. Disgraceful though it might be to yield to a common soldier, the insertion through a chink in the armour of a thin dagger called a misericorde was usually enough to obtain formal surrender, when the captor received a proportion of the ransom and all the captive's armour. The battlefield was not free of trickery, and regulations had to be made covering such eventualities as when a knight was thrown to the ground by one person and another inserted the misericorde and obtained the knight's formal surrender. When that happened, the 'smiter down' was entitled to half the ransom and the one who obtained the surrender received the other half, but he had to take charge of the knight until the ransom was paid. Another battlefield trick was to threaten to kill another man's prisoner unless you were given a share of the ransom. This was frowned upon and, if anyone actually carried out such a threat, he was liable to be arrested by the Marshall and kept in prison until he had paid a fine assessed by the Constable. Another advantage of capturing a knight was that if the captor was a commoner and had no arms of his own, he was allowed to assume those of his captive.

There were some fascinating problems connected with plate armour, especially in later years when it had been perfected. It was then so strong and fitted so closely that it was difficult, if not impossible, to penetrate the joints with a misericorde. James I of England, (1603–25) praising armour, said that it not only protected the wearer, but also prevented him injuring any other person. At the battle of Fornoue a number of Italian knights were thrown to the ground and could not be killed because of the strength of their armour. In the end their captors had to send their servants for heavy woodcutter's axes with which the Italians were finally (and fatally) split open like huge lobsters.

Years later, when plate armour was beginning to go out of fashion, the young Count Christopher von Zedlitz was captured by the Turks in a skirmish outside Vienna, while wearing a cuirass of superb workmanship that must have cost a fortune. The Count was thrown to the ground by the number of his assailants, who when tried to strip him of his armour. Failing to do so, they flung him over a baggage mule and took him back to the Turkish camp, where he was brought before the Grand Vizir. The Grand Vizir ordered the cuirass to be removed, but since the Turks did not wear armour and so had no proper armourers, there was no one present who understood the intricacies of it and so, as the old account has it, 'the Count remained safely esconced in his shell'. The Count was then shown to the Sultan himself, to whom Count Christopher said that if he were promised his life, he would 'undo himself'. The Sultan agreed and the Count then showed the interpreter two tiny screws at the sides of the cuirass and, when these were undone, the cuirass came properly to pieces. The old account of this event continues:

> 'As the report of this spread, there was so much talk in the camp of the Count's feats and of his singular dexterity under that strange attire, that everyone was curious to see him, all the more so as he was one of the first prisoners from the city of Vienna. He was, therefore, ordered to exhibit himself in full curiass, armed at all points for the fight, and to prove whether in this fashion he could without assistance, lift himself from the ground . . . On the following day with mules and several kicking horses being produced, Count Christopher laid himself on the ground

with his curiass screwed up, and, rising nimbly, without any help, sprang on a horse, and repeated this several times; then, with running and vaulting, provided a princely spectacle of knightly exercises . . . When, also, Soliman himself asked him whether, if he should release him, he would still make war on him, Count Christopher answered, undismayed, that if God and his Redeemer should grant him deliverance, he would while life lasted fight against the Turks more hotly than ever. Thereupon the Sultan replied: "Thou shalt be free, my man, and make war on me as thou wilt for the rest of thy life" . . . The Pacha took the Count with him for the first day's march, but in the morning put another Turkish robe of velvet on him over the former, and added a present of a hundred aspers, and also a cavalry prisoner whom the Count knew and had begged for, and caused them to be honourably attended and passed safe, so that on the following day they reached Vienna . . .'

It was allowed, sometimes recommended, to slaughter prisoners of a different religion, but prisoners of the captor's own faith were usually spared. They were stripped of their armour and outer garments, their hands were tied behind their backs and their feet under the belly of the horse on which they were mounted, often blindfold and gagged, to be taken and incarcerated until the ransom money or satisfactory guarantees for it could be obtained. The more important were put in chains, often with neck chains fixed to the wall, for escape meant loss of income; indeed maltreatment, even torture, was thought the best way of screwing the largest amount out of the families of prisoners and getting it quickly. According to the annals of Parma, for instance, 1250 men of Parma were taken prisoner by the combined forces of Cremona and Borgo in 1253. Of these, only 318 were eventually able to redeem their freedom and make their way home. All the others died in captivity before the money for their ransom could be raised, either succumbing to torture — they were made to ride the ghastly wooden horse: two trestles connected by a thin plank of wood set on edge, on which the victim was seated with heavy weights attached to his feet so that within a short time the pain in the victim's crutch became excruciating — or sheer starvation.

Some of the cruelties recorded seem to have been as gratuitous and unmotivated as those of antiquity; for example, in 1151 Friedrich Barbarossa ordered six Milanese prisoners, presumably found to have no assets, to have one eye each put out, six others had their noses cut off up to the forehead and one eye put out, while six others had both eyes put out. According to Richard of Hoveden, Richard Coeur de Lion was capable of equal cruelty: in 1198 he captured 15 French knights, and, to avenge some act of cruelty allegedly performed by the French, ordered 14 of them to have both eyes put out, the last being allowed to retain one eye, so that he could guide them all back to the French army. Philipe Auguste then retaliated by blinding 15 of his English prisoners.

SIEGE WARFARE

By the later Middle Ages warfare had again become largely a matter of besieging and once again belligerents developed a vague code of conduct which was based largely on convenience. When a fortress was unable to offer prolonged resistance or there was little hope of relief from outside, the custom was that, provided the garrison commander surrendered 'on summons', or did not prolong the siege unduly to cause casualities to the besiegers by forcing them to engage in costly assault, the garrison would be granted quarter and honourable terms. A prolonged defence against unreasonable odds could only result in indiscriminate slaughter when the town eventually fell. There was a recognized command for this extreme action: the order 'Havoc!', which, in English armies, was only to be given by the king himself. Shakespeare refers to it in *Julius Caesar*:

> '. . . with a monarch's voice
> Cry "Havoc!" and let slip the dogs of war.'

However, there must have been times when others gave this gruesome order for Article X of the Statutes of Richard II runs 'let no one be so hardy as to cry "Havoc" under pain of losing his head.'

There were acts of clemency, too. When King Alfred (871–99), after defeating the Danes at Ethandun and besieging their camp for a fortnight, had starved them into surrender, he thought it expedient to feed them and set them free. Richard Coeur de Lion was mortally wounded while inspecting the defences of a petty town in France, and when the town subsequently fell, the man who had shot the fatal arrow was brought before the dying king, to whom he insisted that he had only been doing his duty. Richard, faced with the prospect of meeting his Maker, ordered that he be allowed to go free. It was not the king's fault that the moment the breath was out of his body, his soldiers flayed the unfortunate man alive.

There were times when personal, religious or political passions were so inflamed that ransom or compassion of any kind was denied; when it was allowed, even recommended, to slaughter prisoners of different religions or ideologies. On occasion the Greeks slaughtered 'barbarians' whom they had taken prisoner on those very grounds, as the Jews did the Gibeonites, the Arabs those who refused to embrace Islam and the Christians the infidel. The illustrations in the old chronicles of the Turkish wars against Hungary emphasize how captors were expected to send the sultan or his grand vizir the heads of their captives so that these might be counted and the number entered to the credit of the captor in the ledger that would assure him a pleasant time in paradise. Yet when the Knights of St John besieged in Rhodes finally capitulated (1522), although the siege had cost the Turks enormous losses, the Knights were allowed to leave the island with the honours of war, taking their belongings with them. As they marched out, Suleyman sent for their leader and congratulated him on the Knights' galantry and their heroic defence of the city. He even provided them with ships to take them back to Europe.

On the whole, however, killing POWs was for long the common practice when cities were captured. The Thirty Years War provides several examples: Heidelberg, Magdeburg, Kempten, and others. The same can be said of many battles once prisoners of war were no longer sold as slaves, a thing forbidden — where Christians were concerned — by the Third Lateran Council of 1179, although Oliver Cromwell and many others do not appear to have been aware of the fact.

CIVIL WARS

Civil wars have always been the most ruthless and brutal. There is something invidious about capturing your own countrymen. In the Wars of the Roses, Yorkists slaughtered their prisoners of war after Tewkesbury, as the Lancastrians did theirs after Towton, at which 'by mutual agreement no quarter was to be given by either side, and no prisoners were to be taken'. In all 38 000 were killed and one prisoner taken, the Earl of Devonshire, captured 'when they were weary of killing'. During the religious wars between the Huguenots and the Catholic League in France, the château of Ruffec with a garrison of only 50 had to surrender unconditionally to the Catholics, who put them all to the sword. The garrison of Melle, similarly surrendering, met the same fate. On another occasion, the Catholic Commander, the Duc de Joyeuse, a man who had already murdered thousands of Huguenot prisoners, killed wounded on the field of battle, and sacked towns which had been prepared to surrender — all in the name of religion! — finding himself surrounded during the battle of Coutras, threw down his sword and called out that his ransom would be 100 000 crowns. Not even the promise of so huge a sum could tempt the Huguenots who had so much reason to hate him, and he was shot through the head.

The same grim story is repeated down the years: at Dunbar in 1650 Cromwell took 10 000 Scots prisoners; in Ireland he took none. His report on the storming of Drogheda reads:

'. . . our men coming up to them were ordered by me to put them all to the sword . . . and, indeed in the heat of action, I forbade them to spare any that were in arms in the town, and I think that night they put to death about 2000 men.'

Some of the garrison took refuge in St Peter's church and Cromwell later wrote 'I ordered the steeple to be fired, when one of them was heard to say in the midst of the flames: "God damn me, I burn." In the church itself nearly one thousand men were put to the sword.' Cromwell later denied that he had put to death any man not bearing arms, but his despatch states: 'I believe all their friars were knocked on the head but two.' Of the few who finally surrendered, 'when they submitted, their officers were knocked on the head, every tenth man of the soldiers killed, and the rest shipped for the Barbados.'

As the work of conquering Ireland continued, shiploads of prisoners were sent overseas by Cromwell and the government for sale as slaves in Jamaica and the West Indies; the more fortunate, upwards of 40 000 of them, were allowed to enlist for foreign service with the armies of France and Spain. As far as the French were concerned, the Irish proved a mixed blessing, for they lived up to their reputation of being a nuisance in barracks, though extremely effective in the field. 'Your troops,' Louis XV is said to have complained to the commander of the Irish Brigade, 'cause more trouble than the whole of the French army.' 'Your Majesty's enemies, Sire,' came the reply, 'make the same complaint.'

In 1689 it was the turn of those Scots who had refused to recognize William III. Sir William Dalrymple, himself a Scot, wrote to the English commanders: 'I hope the soldiers will not trouble the Government with prisoners.' A hundred and twenty years later, at the battle of Ligny no quarter was given on either side and one of the French generals threatened to shoot anyone who brought in Prussian prisoners.

The French Revolution saw similar atrocities. Prisoners were shot down by the battalion at Lyons and drowned 'by the phalange ' (that is, in large numbers) at Nantes. At Menin a general with his own hand killed wounded emigrés. Defenceless prisoners were killed in the Vendée and the Carlist Wars, by General Hayman in Hungary in 1848, by Radetsky in Italy in the same year, by General Butler in the American War of Independence, in Mexico, and by others elsewhere in many different epochs.

Judging by the accounts of life in the Turkish galleys of the eighteenth and nineteenth centuries or in the Japanese labour camps on the Burma Road in World War II, there is little to choose between them and their

A Turkish army defeated by the French. Three of the victors are holding aloft the severed heads of Turks.

horrors, but there can be no doubt that the worst thing that could happen to a soldier was to be taken prisoner by the Battas of Sumatra. According to Sir Stamford Raffles, the Batta law was that anyone guilty of adultery, midnight robbery or treacherous assault and *all* prisoners of war were to suffer 'death by eating'. The POW was eaten with the least possible delay, almost on the spot:

> 'The captive is tied to a stake, with his arms extended: the chief enemy has the first selection, and after he has cut off his slice, others cut off pieces, according to their taste or fancy, until all the flesh is devoured. It is eaten either raw or grilled, with a mixed condiment of chili pepper and salt.'

There are various accounts of life in the Turkish galleys, which probably was little different from that of their predecessors who manned the sweeps of the Roman ships. For either, the most likely form of release was death; though occasionally a Turkish galley or one of those used by the Barbary pirates would be captured and the people released. One of these lucky ones was Baron Wencelaus Wratislaw, who was captured as a young man and sent to the galleys. Somehow he survived and on his release wrote an account of his life there:

> 'The vessel was tolerably large, and in it five prisoners sat on a bench, pulling together at a single oar. It is incredible how great the misery of rowing in the galleys is: no work in the world can be harder; for they chain each prisoner by one foot under his seat, leaving him so far free to move that he can get on the bench and pull the oar. When they are rowing, it is impossible, on account of the great heat, to pull otherwise than naked, without any upper clothing, and with nothing on the whole body but a pair of linen trousers. When such a boat sails through the Dardanelles, out of the narrow into the broad sea, iron bracelets or rings, are immediately passed over the hands of each captive, so that they may not be able to resist and defend themselves against the Turks. And, thus fettered hand and foot the captive must row day and night, unless there is a gale, till the skin on his back is scorched like that of a singed hog, and cracks from the heat. The sweat flows into the eyes and steeps the whole body, whence arises excessive agony, especially to silken hands unaccustomed to work, on which blisters are formed from the oars and yet give way to the oar one must: for when the superintendent sees anyone taking breath, and resting, he immediately beats him, naked as he is, either with the usual galley-slave scourge, or with a wet rope dipped in the sea, till he makes abundance of bloody weals over his whole body . . . for food nothing is given but two small cakes of biscuit . . . Indeed, we had a most miserable, sorrowful life, and worse than death, in that vessel.'

EXCHANGE AND RANSOMING

The best that the POW of antiquity (ie. of the ancient world, including Greece and Rome) could have hoped for was to be allowed to go free; when, if not too far from home, he would have a chance of making his way there. Another possibility was exchange. Small states, such as Sparta, had so few fighting men that they were always eager to get them back by exchange or ransoming. If neither exchanged nor ransomed, you might be sold into slavery or kept by your captor as his slave. The word 'slave' has a nasty ring in the ears of those who remember the slave labour camps of the Russians and Nazis, but down the ages those who have paid good money for a slave have mostly been reasonably solicitous of their purchase and provided him or her with food, shelter and most of their wants. In ancient Greece and Rome many slaves made a comfortable living as cooks, scribes, and doctors, while more than a few made fortunes as charioteers or gladiators.

It was exceptional that a victor had no use for his captives and so slaughtered them. This occurred in less than one in four of the battles recorded in Greek history. In later centuries, the slaughter of prisoners became more frequent, especially in civil wars or when fanaticism (political or religious) was a factor. There was then almost an unwritten obligation on the victor to slaughter prisoners of a different faith, unless they were willing to renounce their own faith and embrace the captor's. Others have killed prisoners just because they did not know what to do with them. In *Why they collaborated* Eugene Kinkhead quotes US Colonel Willis Perry as telling him:

> 'In the first five months of the (Korean) war, North Koreans had often shot soldiers they could have taken prisoner, or had shot prisoners while combat conditions still existed in the immediate area, simply because they did not want to bother with them. They were completely unprepared, on the whole, to handle prisoners. They had little food to give them and what they had was often bad; and they had no place to put them . . .'

Those most eager to invite their prisoners to embrace the faith of their captors were the Saracens and, 5–600 years later, the opponents of the Western presence in India, especially Hyder Ali and Typpoo Sahib. This invitation always contained an element of compulsion, but sometimes there was not even an element of invitation, just a command backed up by force. This, in eighteenth-century India, was known as 'Mohammedanization', the process being vividly described by one of its victims, James Scurry, who together with 51 others (the oldest of whom was 17, the youngest 12) had been segregated and for several weeks kept apart from the other prisoners, being well fed and treated with exceptional kindness (when any kindness at all was exceptional). They were next persuaded to have their heads shaved without being told why this was required, and then, as James Scurry himself relates:

> 'This being done, they left us to ourselves another week, when, one morning, the same barbers came with twelve of the most robust men I ever saw; these were some of Hyder's *getiees*, all from Madagascar, kept by him for feats of strength and agility. . . . Their appearance told us plainly that something was going on, although we could not form any opinion of the object which they had in view; but the arrival of Dempster, the name of the European before alluded to, once more unravelled the mystery. He addressed us in the most endearing, though hypocritical language, and gave us to understand, that we were to be circumcised, and made Mohammedans of, by the express order of Hyder. We were thunderstruck, but what could be done?
> . . . They forced each of us to take a quantity of majum, a drug well calculated to stupefy the senses and deaden pain; but it had little effect this latter way.
> A mat, and a kind of sheet, being provided for each of us, we were ordered to arrange ourselves in two rows, and then lie down on our mats. This being done, the guards, barbers and those twelve men before-mentioned, came among us, and seizing the youngest, Randal

Cadman, midshipman, they placed him on a cudgeree pot, when four of these stout men held his legs and arms, while the barber performed his office. In this manner they went through the operation, and in two hours the *pious* work was finished, and we were laid on our separate mats; where, with the effects of the majum, some were laughing, and others crying; which, together with the pain, rendered our condition truly curious and ludicrous . . .

During our illness, or rather soreness, the clothes we had worn were taken from us, and coarse habits given us; but we were not even yet completely Mohammedanized . . . Four large coppers were brought into the square, accompanied by facquars or priests, worstards or schoolmasters, and a religious train, to consummate the business and make us genuine children of the Prophet. Each copper would, at least, contain one hogshead and a half of water, which was made unusually warm. The reason was, as we understood afterwards, that we had eaten a great quantity of pork in our time, and consequently were very unclean. Here was no small diversion for idle spectators, to see us jump out of the coppers half scalded; the facquars in the midst of their prayers, suspending their ceremonies, and joining the guards in running after and bringing us back; for, by the time two were taken, they would be in pursuit of two more, who had made their escape from this terrific ordeal. In this we found some advantage; for during our short absence the water naturally cooled . . .'

INDOCTRINA- TION, ANCIENT AND MODERN

This part of the proceedings occupied three days, after which we were hailed as true children of the Prophet, and the favourites of the Nabob.'

This wish to convert the 'unbeliever' to one's own faith was probably prompted in part by the realization of the divisive effect of having people of different faiths living in the same community; also, in the captor's eyes, he was doing them a service by saving their souls. In modern times, which have seen the emergence of a new religion, Communism, the very considerable efforts of its adherents in this direction have been purely political, in fact a covert form of warfare. In World War II the Russians practiced it most notoriously and with conspicuous lack of success on the 8500 Polish soldiers, mostly officers, whom the Russian security forces gathered in three camps after the Soviet annexation of Eastern Poland in 1939. These were mostly reservists, professional men and intellectuals, recalled to the colours in the general mobilization of the last few weeks of peace.

The Soviet object was to select men to train to officer a Red Polish army they hoped to raise and also to provide political leaders for the future. The method employed was basically endless interrogation, up to 72 hours at a stretch, spiced with intimidation and torture, the object being to emphasize the sense of defeat that the Poles obviously felt, to fill them with doubts as to the future and the rightness of what had gone before, and by forbidding any public manifestation of religious worship, to make them feel that not even God was with them. Despite the immense effort put into this endeavour, the 'harvest' consisted of some 20 candidates for the thousands of vacant posts.

Of these the world has heard of only one, Colonel Zygmunt Berling, who became commander of the so-called Kosciuszko Division, and whose name is now linked with that of the Norwegian traitor and Nazi stooge, Quisling. The others, whom the Soviets had not been able to persuade to forget that they were Poles and that Russia was their country's arch- and traditional enemy, were liquidated either in the forest at Katyn or in the waters of the White Sea. (It was not until the Allies had publicly admitted that they were not going to be able to help Poland regain her freedom and were abandoning her to the Russians that realism forced the Poles to accept their conquerors' conditions and service.)

Conversion to the Communist faith was adopted as a weapon of warfare, continuing even after hostilities had ceased, by the Russians, Koreans and Chinese, the idea being that if POWs could be sent back believing in the Communist doctrine they could help either by spreading the gospel in their own country or by becoming 'sleepers' who would act as saboteurs or fifth-columnists when the time came. The Soviets were the first in the field with their Antifa (Antifascist) organization, which sought its pupils from among the hundreds of thousands of German POWs who were being retained to labour for the victors as part of reparations, those who learned their lessons properly being rewarded with earlier repatriation. This organization began work in January 1946, after the Potsdam Declaration, at the end of the Three Power Conference of August 1945, to the effect that 'The Allies wish to make it possible for the German people to prepare to build their lives again on the basis of democracy and peace . . .'. Not that the Soviets had any such desire, for the lessons they taught were anti-capitalist rather than anti-fascist and their burden that the Western Allies, above all the USA, were their country's (Germany's) bitterest and most dangerous enemies, and that Germany would do much better to embrace Russian social dogma.

The British and the Americans both had programmes of reeducation or denazification of their German POWs, but as those who have real faith are seldom to be converted, and where there is no real faith there is no need for conversion, these efforts were largely a waste of time.

Those who most eagerly assumed the mantle of the Spanish Inquisition were the Chinese and Korean communists, themselves recent converts and thus especially rabid. A great deal of research into their methods and their effectiveness has resulted in a number of books, but it would seem that the whole procedure with its mixture of stick, carrot and public confession is so labour-intensive that it ties up many more men than required just to guard the prisoners. This might perhaps be justified, if the method had proved successful, but the statistics now available seem to prove that brainwashing (of the adult) carried out in this way, is as ineffectual as it is cruel, especially when practiced on people of a different race.

In earlier wars, especially in those waged when Islam was still a rela-tively youthful force, the Mohammedan captor was often in too much of a hurry to issue an invitation to change faith; there was, after all, kudos and profit too to be had from providing the vizir or sultan with the heads of Christians. In his account of the seventeenth-century siege of Belgrade, Monsieur de la Colonie has described how the Turks:

> 'suddenly rushed at us sword in hand, in no formation whatever, uttering the most frightful yells, and then threw themselves upon our people, whom they completely surrounded, front and flanks, with the result that all, excepting some few who happened to be more in the rear and who took to their heels in time, were slain and decapitated, including poor M. de Margilly. The little cavalry detachment was ready at the first alarm, but had hardly moved a pace in advance when a cannon ball fired from one of the caiques carried away their colonel . . . The lieutenant-colonel, however, led them on, but the Turks, who never stay long upon one spot, and who carry out their designs with great promptitude when they have taken them in hand, had made off,

laden with the heads of our people. According to their custom, a ducat is given for every Christian head brought in by their soldiers, which profit tends to animate them in the fight.'

History seems to show that, unless you can get a reasonable price or ransom for him, the prisoner of war is wanted by nobody. But, having got him, you have to feed and house him, not always easy by any means, and thus it is logical that you should make use of him in one way or another. You can use his labour for a limited length of time; you can try to indoctrinate him with your philosophy and send him home to act as a subversive agent; or you can try to assimilate him into your own society. This, perhaps, is what Typpoo Sahib was trying to do with James Scurry and the other young Britishers serving in the armies of the East India Company whom he had captured. Not that Typpoo was a humanitarian, for Scurry records that 'It was not infrequently that two or three hundred noses and ears would be exhibited in the public market, but to whom they belonged we could not learn'. However, that is not the way he treated Scurry and his fellow Britishers, who, as Scurry relates:

'We were one day strangely informed that each of us, who was of proper age, was to have a wife; for this piece of news we were extremely sorry, (Scurry wrote this account after his return to England and his marriage to an English girl, so he may well have been less than honest here) but there was no possibility of our preventing their designs. There were at this time, a number of young girls, who had been driven with their relations out of the Carnatic . . . some of these poor creatures were allotted to us; and one morning, we were ordered to fall into rank and file, when those girls were placed one behind each of us, while we stood gazing at one another, wondering what they were about to do. At last, the *durga* gave the word. "To the right about face", with the addition (in the Moorish language) of "Take what is before you". This, when understood, some did, and some did not; but the refractory were soon obliged to comply . . . Two months passed on, when the priest came to consummate our nuptials: the bride and her escort were led to an eminence, with flowers round their necks, and seated; after which, their thumbs were tied together, the priest muttering something which we could not comprehend, and we were married. They, however, gave us to understand that we were subject to pay eighty rupees to the cadi, in case we divorced our wives, very few of whom exceeded eleven years of age . . .'

Such methods of persuasion might have been expected to be more effective than brainwashing or torture, but after having two children by his young wife, Scurry escaped, abandoning them, and made his way back to the East India Company's forces and so eventually to England. Maybe it is impossible to make a leopard change its spots. Today, so near the end of the twentieth century, it would seem that the POW has himself became a potential weapon which can be used against his own side. Just as in medieval warfare an archer would pick up those of the enemy's arrows that had missed their mark and shoot them back at him, so today, a side waging a political war takes the enemies it captures and tries to convert them to its own beliefs, turning them into weapons of subversion that can eventually be returned to their own country there to fight for their erstwhile captor. The concept that the prisoner of war is a poor devil, 'a passive human being in need of care and protection' has gone, perhaps, for ever.

The POW today

Arab prisoners at Sharm el Sheikh, the Egyptian fortress controlling the Strait of Tiran, after its capture by Israeli forces. The Middle East offers an interesting footnote to the history of the POW. The only example of a POW receiving a reward is that of the modern Iraqi who has been captured by the Iranians. His children, brothers and sisters will automatically be credited with five points in the totting up system used in Iraq for university entrance (no vulgar question of academic ability here!) and, once at university, they will be allowed to fail their exams for three years in succession, before being required to leave.

The status of the POW in international law was finally fixed to everyone's satisfaction in 1949, though by no means all countries of the world have signed the relevant convention. All that has happened since then to change the situation is that the US, French and others have issued instructions to their armed forces that it is the duty of those who have been captured and made prisoners of war to do their utmost to escape and rejoin their own forces. Such prisoners cannot strictly be regarded as no longer taking an active

part in the war. Although they do not have weapons in their hands, they are to some extent still fighting, and thus how they are treated is still open to question.

The regulations concerning the conditions under which POWs are to be kept and their treatment generally set out in the convention are the ideal, possible to provide in times of peace but often quite impracticable in wartime with all its shortages and logistic difficulties, the same in every war, problems that will not go away.

CHAPTER 2

STATUS OF THE POW

It was not until 1907 that the POW acquired a status in international law. Before that as we have seen he often had a financial value in that he could be employed as a slave or sold to himself (ransom) or anyone else with the money to buy him; where neither was possible he was an unwanted nuisance, who having no rights was often disposed of according to the convenience of his captor. When both sides had taken prisoners, his fate was often determined by the principle of tit-for-tat. If one side killed prisoners, so did the other; if one side cut rations, so did the other; and so on. In the age of reason, or as some historians have called it the age of common sense, war was waged with a degree of humanity unmatched before or since. The campaigns in the wars between the French and English in the eighteenth century were really personal quarrels between their kings and employed only regular soldiers, and so it was not difficult to wage war to the accepted rules of their profession and confine its effects to the combatants. If prisoners were taken, they were regarded as fellows in arms towards whom no rancour or enmity was felt, and they were amicably disposed of by exchange, each country sending the other a bill for what it had spent on food and clothing for the captives.

Before this, during the sixteenth century, people had become increasingly aware of the need for a code of conduct towards prisoners of war and conquered civilians. The first steps towards this were not international agreements, but specific to the particular belligerents in a particular war, the first probably being the treaty of 1581 between Tournay and the Prince of Parma, which provided for the free withdrawal of the garrison of Tournay including their wounded. Then in 1637 came the first serious suggestion of modern times that those who surrendered should not be put to death if unable to pay a ransom. This was made by the French writer Gabriel Naudé.

In 1689, a cartel for the exchange and ransom of prisoners of war was concluded between France and Spain. The system of exchange — almost as old as war itself — was humane, civilized and eminently sensible, and it was praised by the famous international jurist Vattel who in 1758 when Britain and France were at war wrote:

> 'We praise the English and French. Our hearts glow with love for them when we hear how prisoners of war, on both sides, are treated by these generous nations.'

The object of taking and keeping prisoners of war being solely to deprive the opponent of his fighting efficiency, it was recognized that there was no reason why those who gave their word not to engage in further hostilities should not be allowed to live as free people or with very few restrictions, if they could pay for accommodation, until an exchange could be arranged. This was applied originally only to officers, though more recently the system of exchange has operated throughout all ranks, from general officer to private soldier; and on the whole there has been no cheating by sending back an unequal number of prisoners.

The greatest possible trust has always been placed on an officer's honour, so that those who accepted parole need not wait in captivity until an exchange could be arranged. They were free to live where they liked, in some cases even to return to their own country and family, provided that they had given their word not to serve in the armed forces until they had been notified that an exchange had been effected — that is to say, an enemy officer of equal rank had been captured and released by the opposite side. To break parole was an unforgivable sin. An officer who did so would be ostracized, probably cashiered, and even sent back to the enemy's country to be deservedly confined. The only justification for breaking parole and escaping from an enemy country was if the enemy had first broken his word by placing the prisoner in confinement and not treating him as a man of honour. An agreement was made in 1780 between England and France which laid down the rates for ransom for all ranks. (There do not, however, appear to have been many cases of people buying their liberty rather than waiting for an exchange.)

Probably the first agreement between nations as to the actual treatment of prisoners in captivity also belongs to the enlightened eighteenth century. This was embodied in a Treaty of Friendship made in 1785 between Prussia and the United States. It forbade confinement in civil convict prisons and the use of fetters, and required that prisoners should have adequate rations on the scale of the captor nation's own troops, and sufficient exercise for good health. Since the two countries never went to war with each other, such an agreement proved unnecessary, but it illustrates the humanitarian impulse of the times, particularly as far as the 'other ranks' were concerned, as they could not give parole and would have to wait in confinement until exchanged in batches.

NAPOLEON AND EXCHANGE

In this most civilized of all periods of European history, war was conducted with absolute mutual trust; but it was never to be so again. The French Revolution in 1789, and the substitution of nations in arms for small professional armies, began to weaken the eighteenth century structure of the 'gentleman's war', and Napoleon pulled it to the ground. He was, alas, no gentleman.

At the outbreak of hostilities after the Revolution, France's policy was

Prisoners being marched
away in 1759.

'All governments are our enemies; all peoples are our allies'. Any Frenchman who maltreated a prisoner would be, it was proclaimed, as guilty as if he
had assaulted a fellow Frenchman. In 1801, the French jurist and statesman
Portalis advocated the theory, originated earlier by Rousseau, that war con-
cerns only the armed forces of the belligerents and that the peoples of
warring states are enemies only as soldiers and not as civilians. This had in
effect been the position throughout the eighteenth century, because even
when England and France were at war, there were colonies of English residents in France, the English travelled in and through France on the Grand
Tour and a cross-channel service still operated (though until the peace of
Amiens, which was in effect a 'half-time' interval in the Napoleonic Wars,
not many English had wished to visit France once the old régime had
collapsed). As soon, however, as peace was declared and even before it was
actually signed, the wealthy English flocked back to the Continent, all
unsuspecting of what was in store for them. On May 18, 1803 England
declared war again, since Napoleon's preparations and extortionate
demands, which included the return of all French refugees in Britain, made
a resumption of hostilities inevitable. On May 23 Napoleon ordered the
arrest of every Englishman on French soil between the ages of 18 and 60. His
haul included a large proportion of the House of Lords.

Napoleon's excuse for this move was the seizure by the British fleet of
some small French ships in their own home waters before, he claimed,
hostilities had commenced. He consequently claimed that the English
civilians were 'hostages', though later modifying this and adopting the
argument that since every Englishman was liable to serve in the militia
between these ages, every one of his prisoners was a potential militiaman.
They would therefore count with regular troops in any exchanges. For year
after year negotiations of some agreed method of exchange continued,
Napoleon continually raising his demands: the Hanoverians and Spaniards
among his captives were to be included for trading purposes; this or that

condition had to be observed; promises were made, only to be withdrawn. A few individual exchanges did take place, but in reality the system of exchange as a whole was dead.

The treatment of those who surrendered in the field appears to have been based on mutual expediency rather than law. Writing to his brother Lord Wellesley in 1810 during the Peninsular Campaign, the Duke of Wellington remarked:

> 'Since I have commanded the troops in this country, I have always treated the French officers and soldiers, who have been made prisoner, with the utmost humanity and attention, and in numerous instances I have saved their lives. The only motive which I have had for this conduct has been that they might treat our officers and soldiers well, who might fall into their hands, and I must do the French justice to say that they have been universally well treated.'

Wellington may not have known what was in store for his prisoners, when they finally arrived at such places of detention as Dartmoor and the hulks. As every soldier who has had the misfortune to be taken prisoner knows, 'the further down the line, the more bloody minded the treatment', and the greater the problem the POW poses, especially when numbers are really large.

As late as the nineteenth century, international agreement on the treatment of prisoners of war and even on the definition of a prisoner of war was as far away as ever. The founder of the International Red Cross Henri Dunant vainly tried to include treatment of prisoners of war in the Geneva Convention, and it was not until the present century that any real progress was made. The Hague Convention of 1907 laid down fairly extensive rules regarding prisoners of war, and these were in operation during World War I. They proved inadequate and were revised in 1929. World War II showed clearly that still more was needed and further amendments were made in 1949.

The regulations of 1929 were in force between all combatant nations during World War II, except Germany and Russia; however, the War Crimes Tribunal upheld the view that the fact that a nation does not subscribe to the Hague Convention does not mean that it can be disregarded.

Since 1949 the categories of those who after they have fallen into the hands of the enemy must be treated as prisoners of war are:

1. Members of the armed forces of a party to the conflict as well as members of militias or volunteer corps forming part of such forces.
2. Members of other militias and members of other volunteer corps including those of organized resistance movements belonging to a party to the conflict and operating in or outside their own territory, even if this territory is occupied, provided that such militias or volunteer corps, including such organized resistance movements, fulfil the following conditions: that of being commanded by a person responsible for his subordinates; that of having a fixed distinctive sign recognizable at a distance; that of carrying arms openly; that of conducting their operations in accordance with the laws and customs of war.
3. Members of regular armed forces who profess allegiance to a government or an authority not recognized by the Detaining Power.
4. Persons who accompany the armed forces without actually being members thereof (eg war correspondents, members of labour and welfare

The main regulations governing the treatment of POWs

The rules and regulations are the result of much thought on the part of humane men of good will. The experience of two world wars and many lesser ones has shown that circumstances are often such that with the best will in the world it is physically impossible to treat prisoners in the way the regulations require. When numbers are small it is seldom difficult to comply with them, but when numbers are large it is usually impossible to do so.

No form of coercion may be inflicted on prisoners to induce them to provide information other than their surname, date of birth, and army, regimental, personal or serial number, which they are obliged to furnish.

Prisoners are entitled to retain all their personal belongings, including badges of rank and decorations, but not arms or military equipment.

Prisoners must be removed from the danger area as soon as possible after capture.

Prisoners must be given food and water and all reasonable precautions taken to ensure their safety.

Immediately after capture a prisoner is to be allowed to write directly to his family and to the Central Prisoners of War Agency. Thereafter he must be allowed to send at least two letters and four cards every month. He must be allowed to receive parcels of food, clothing, medical supplies and articles of a religious, educational or recreational nature.

Prisoners are to be grouped according to nationality, language and customs, and are not to be separated from those of the armed force with which they were serving when captured, without their consent.

Camps for prisoners must be outside the combat zone and not in the proximity of military installations. Bomb shelters must be provided and the prisoners allowed to use them.

Conditions (size of dormitories, bedding, heating) under which prisoners are kept must be as good as those of the troops of the Detaining Power. Food must be sufficient, relative to the prisoners' habitual diet, to maintain good health. They must have a sufficiency of drinking water.

The Detaining Power must see that the prisoners are and remain properly clothed. There must be canteens at which prisoners can obtain soap, tobacco, food and everyday articles at prices not above those prevailing locally. Each camp must have an adequate infirmary where they can have special care and diet.

Prisoners qualified as doctors, dentists etc may be required to act as such, and are then not to be considered as prisoners of war. They and ministers of religion are to be allowed to visit prisoners working outside a camp.

Discipline in camps is to be the responsibility of a regular officer of the forces of the detaining power. He must possess a copy of the Convention and it is his duty to see that its provisions are known to the camp guards and staff.

A Detaining Power may use the labour of prisoners of war who are physically fit, but NCOs shall only be required to do supervisory work, though they may apply for work. Officers may not to be compelled to work under any circumstances, but they may ask for work. Only work of the following categories shall be done: agriculture; production or extraction of raw materials, manufacture (but not metallurgy, machinery or chemical industries); public works and building works of no military character or purpose; transport and handling of non-military stores; commerce, arts and crafts, domestic service, public utility services of non-military character. Unless they volunteer, prisoners shall not be employed on work that is humiliating, unhealthy or dangerous, nor shall they have to work longer hours than the maximum permitted for civilian labourers. All work is to be paid for at a fair working rate.

Prisoners may make complaints direct to the Protecting Power or through the prisoners' representatives, and they must not be punished for doing so. Prisoners' representatives are elected by ballot every six months and are to be of the same nationality, language and customs as those they represent.

A prisoner is subject to the law in

The Convention lays it down that POWs must be kept in a place of safety, of which there are none left in the world. This POW is being made to dig a slit trench for his own protection in the event of an air raid by his own side.

force in the armed forces of the Detaining Power which may take disciplinary measures for any offence against them. Trial is to be by military court, unless the laws of the detaining power expressly give jurisdiction to the civil authority. A prisoner is entitled to defend himself or be given defending counsel. No one may be punished twice for the same act.

Torture, corporal punishment, imprisonment in premises without daylight and collective punishment for individual acts are forbidden, as is humiliating and degrading treatment.

An attempt to escape entails a disciplinary punishment only, though the offender may be subject to special surveillance thereafter. Offences committed solely in order to escape and which do not involve violence against life or limb are subject to disciplinary punishment only. Other prisoners who aid or abet an escape shall be subject to disciplinary punishment only. Prisoners who have succeeded in escaping, but are subsequently recaptured are not liable to punishment for their first escape.

The invention of the steamship

allowed POWs to be sent out of harm's way to safe and salubrious places with ease and despatch, eg the Boer War.

The invention of the aeroplane, whose early shortcomings often meant that it had to make a forced landing in enemy territory, introduced a new facet of capture. If the plane landed near enemy troops, capture of the crew would be more or less immediate; but, if there were no troops in the vicinity, the crew, if uninjured, might have an opportunity to escape before they were captured. If the plane was a bomber, the crew were sometimes exposed to the wrath of the civilian population.

The invention of the telephone and wireless made it easy to send news of an escape — now even a picture of the escaper — far and wide.

World War II introduced the concept of the war crime, according to which the fact that a soldier, whatever his rank, has received an order to perpetrate an atrocity, does not exonerate him from the consequences of having done so. The idea of 'his not to reason why, his but to do and die' is now obsolete.

The UN Command conducting operations in Korea established the principle that a POW does not have to be repatriated at the end of hostilities, if he does not wish to go home.

The advent of proselytizing Communism has meant that the prisoner taken by Communist forces has been subjected to a new form of non-physical attack: indoctrination. The object of this is to recruit the POW by persuading him of the rightness of his captor's philosophy and then to repatriate him at the end of hostilities to be an active protagonist of his captor's cause in his home country.

The fact that USA, France and other countries take the view that a member of their armed forces who is captured, does not give up the struggle, but is duty bound to try to escape and rejoin his own forces, means that today a POW has not surrendered or 'made an offer of peace', he has merely laid down his arms temporarily and will try to take up others, ie he is still actively fighting. This is an idea with wide implications.

units, etc), provided that they have received authorization from the armed forces which they accompany, who shall provide them for that purpose with an identity card similar to the annexed model.

5. Members and crews, including masters, pilots and apprentices of the merchant marine and crews of civil aircraft and of the parties to the conflict, who do not benefit by more favourable treatment under any other provisions of International Law.

6. Inhabitants of a nonoccupied territory who, on the approach of the enemy, spontaneously take up arms to resist the invading forces without having had time to form themselves into regular armed units, provided they carry arms openly and respect the laws and customs of war.

The Convention goes to the utmost length to include practically every type of combatant and uses great ingenuity to do so. It appeared that the only types of enemy subject who could be shot as criminals would be a man operating on his own, wearing no identifying sign such as an armband, and using a knife or pistol which he had concealed, or collectively those in occupied territory who threaten the safety of the occupying power, such threats being spying, sabotage or murder.

Is it possible for laws, however definite and unequivocal, to take the place of a code of usage devised by professional soldiers and based on a common respect for each other? Is 'common humanity' possible in any war which includes the bombing of civilians, unrestricted submarine warfare, slaughter and deportation of civilians? To pass laws against murder or theft will not prevent these acts. The perpetrator only suffers if he is caught. By the same token the military commander who orders or allows atrocities contrary to international law will know that he may face a War Crimes Tribunal if he loses — but what if he wins?

How interpret such laws in any case? Consider the categories of those who, if captured, are to be regarded as prisoners of war. The greatest difficulty is the definition of 'organized resistance movements' (Clause 2), further confused by Clause 6 which includes unorganized combatants — those who 'spontaneously' take up arms 'without having had time to form themselves into regular armed units'. What is 'a person responsible for his subordinates'? Does this mean appointed from above, or elected from below by his comrades? At what distance must the 'fixed distinctive emblem' be recognizable? It has been suggested that, under the rules of land warfare, 'it is reasonable to expect that the silhouette of an irregular combatant standing against the skyline should be at once distinguishable from that of a peaceful inhabitant by the naked eye of ordinary individuals, at a distance at which the form of an individual can be determined' (*International Law*, Vol 2 L Oppenheim, 7th edition). This presumably means in broad daylight. If this is the case, partisans and Home Guards had best not surrender!

YOUR PAPERS OR YOUR LIFE

The problem of irregular combatants has increased enormously with the rapid advances of mechanized forces. In the Franco-Prussian War, the Germans had difficulties with civilian fighters and adopted a simple method of dealing with them. If the *franc tireur* could produce an individual authorization from the French Government, he was taken prisoner; if not, he was shot. It may be cynical to wonder how often such individuals were asked to produce their papers. In the occupied territories during World War II, the 'civilian' fighter had his heyday — partisans, maquis, chetniks, resistance fighters — or, regrettably, plain assassins.

Of the making of laws there is no end, but neither usages of war, nor international conventions, nor the normal laws of humanity, will prevent what are afterwards considered to be atrocities, if men's anger is aroused beyond the limit of restraint, or if the policy of the nation or its contempt for human life (particularly that of a prisoner) dictates that a course of brutality shall be followed.

The German view of this problem was conveyed by the saying: *Kriegsräson geht vor Kriegsmanier*; in war, need comes before usage. Clausewitz, the military philospher expressed it another way:

> 'Violence arms itself with the inventions of art and science in order to contend against violence. Self-imposed restrictions, almost imperceptible and hardly worth mentioning, termed usages of international war, accompany it without essentially impairing its power'.

If, therefore, a country believes that any form of violence is allowable in war, it is equally necessary that its troops should be brutalized as soldiers. Again, if the troops are to be brutalized, the officer must be above the law, and the army regarded as entirely apart from the civilian population. Hence the almost incredible traditions of the nineteenth-century Prussian officer corps which not only allowed an officer to cut down a civilian who obstructed him in the street, but if he failed to do so would cashier him for having failed to avenge his honour.

At the Hague Conference of 1907, the German plenipotentiary not only agreed to all proposals, but acutally suggested that they did not go far enough. Events proved this to be hypocritical, for whereas the British subsequently produced a *Manual of Military Law* which included every clause of the Convention and made them binding on all officers, the Germans had in their service manual *Kriegsbrauch im Landkriege* (1902), issued to all officers, accepted that 'prisoners can be killed . . . in cases of extreme necessity, when other means of security are not available and the presence of the prisoners is a danger to one's own existence . . .'

The American Instructions of 1863, art 60 reads: '. . . in great straits, when his own salvation makes it impossible to cumber himself with prisoners' a commander is at liberty to kill his prisoners. To do so is certainly ugly, but common sense would seem on occasion to require that it be done. Only the armchair combatant legislating in times of peace can seriously expect a commander to endanger the lives of his own men to save those of enemies who until quite recently were doing their best to kill him.

SURRENDER AND SLAUGHTER

It is, of course, extraordinarily difficult to judge when POWs have become a threat to security and in war there is never time to 'wait and see'. In September 1396 there was the infamous instance of the Crusaders, aware (like their prisoners) of the imminent arrival of a huge Sultan's army to relieve Nicopolis. The Crusaders massacred the thousand Turkish and Bulgarian prisoners of noble birth whom they had previously captured at Rachowa and were holding to ransom. Such men, as yet undebilitated by captivity, could well have constituted a danger, but did they? We shall never know, but as contemporary chroniclers damned the massacre as barbaric, the probability is that they did not. This act of barbarism elicited the obvious response from the victorious Turks after they had defeated the Crusaders in the subsequent battle. They set about slaughtering the Crusaders (who were Frenchmen), although the Turkish soldiery hid quite a number and subsequently sold them as slaves. The only ones spared were those of high station and income (who were allowed to buy their own freedom) and anyone who was obviously under the age of 20. There is a graphic description of how Bajazet, sitting under an awning surrounded by his staff, had the Christians, 'in chains, tightly bound with cords and stripped down to their doublets,' brought before him. This 'enemy of the (Christian) faith' gave each a brief scrutiny and then signed to the executioners who either seized the captive and 'struck them horribly about the head, chest and back, slaughtering them without pity', or set them apart for ransoming, when they were sent with the Sultan's share of the prisoners to Galipoli.

It was because he was unable to feed his prisoners after taking Jaffa that Napoleon had 2000 Arnauts killed, as he did not wish to release them and so increase the enemy's strength. The British, in the same circumstances during the Boer War, *did* release their prisoners; but then, as has been said before, Napoleon was no gentleman.

Today, the Oriental attitude is utterly different to that of the Western nations on many of these questions. Yet, in one respect, the Oriental mind thinks like Plato, who in his *Republic* stated that the soldier who gave up fighting deserved whatever happened to him, a view that seems to have been shared by the Romans a hundred years later. According to Eutropius, the senate decreed that all Roman soldiers captured by Pyrrhus and subsequently released were to be declared 'dishonoured', because they had let themselves be taken prisoner while bearing arms, and they were not to be rehabilitated until they had produced the equipment of two enemy soldiers killed by their own hand. The modern Soviet Russian also takes the view that capture in battle is infamous. It is recorded that Hitler told the captain of his escort flight Hans Bauer that Stalin had said in reply to a request for an

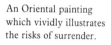
An Oriental painting which vividly illustrates the risks of surrender.

exchange of arrangements for POWs: 'There are no Russian POWs. The Russian soldier fights on till death. If he chooses to become a prisoner, he is automatically excluded from the Russian community.'

This too was the modern Japanese view. In *Defeat into Victory*, the late Field Marshall the Viscount Slim wrote: 'If five hundred Japanese were ordered to hold a position we had to kill four hundred and ninety-five before it was ours — and the last five killed themselves.' A most revealing example of the Japanese belief that a prisoner who had fought well *deserved* death rather than captivity (the opposite of the Port Arthur capitulation terms) is illustrated by the fate of ten survivors of a raiding party of 23, including seven officers, who had attempted to blow up vessels in the harbour of Singapore in September 1944. The attempt failed, but the raiders fought from island to island until the survivors were captured. They were regarded with great respect by their Japanese captors and subsequently put on trial. It is the speech of the prosecuting officer at their trial which is so revealing:

> 'When the deed is so heroic, its sublime spirit must be respected, and its success or failure becomes a secondary matter. These heroes must have left Australia with sublime patriotism flaming in their breasts, and with the confident expectation of all the Australian people on their shoulders. The last moment of a hero must be heroic and it must be dramatic. Heroes have more regard for their reputation than for anything else. As we respect them, so we feel our duty for glorifying their last moments as they deserve, and by our doing so the names of these heroes will remain in the heart of the British and Australian people for evermore. I consider that a death sentence should be given to each of the accused.'

They were duly executed on July 7, 1945.

Contrast this with the terms of capitulation given to the Russian garrison of Port Arthur, when it surrendered to the Japanese in 1905 when Japan was a signatory to the 1899 Convention. Article 7, for instance (the terms were all written in English), was:

> 'The Japanese army will, in honour of the gallant defence made by the Russians, allow the Russian military and naval officers, as well as the civil officials attached to the Russian army and navy, to wear swords and to take with them such personal effects as may be necessary for their subsistence. With regard to the above mentioned officers, officials and volunteers the Japanese army will permit them to go home if they subscribe to a written oath not to take up arms until the close of the war, and to refrain from doing any action whatever inconsistent with the interest of the Japanese army. Every such military and naval officer shall be allowed to take with him an orderly who shall be specially released on parole.'

RISKING SURRENDER

In 1920 the International Law Association recommended that the 'laying-down of arms' be recognized as an 'offer of peace' that must be accepted. There are, however, circumstances in which surrender cannot be accepted, because to do so will endanger the victor's own safety (not enough water, food, being grossly outnumbered, or in naval warfare, the fact that so many extra bodies on board would sink the ship). This, however, has never been accepted by the international lawmaker, whose humanitarian instincts seem stronger than his ability to recognize realities, such as those facing the Greek

A scene from the Nuremberg Trials at which it was internationally accepted that being ordered to commit an atrocity did not exonerate private or general from having done so. Before surrender, refusal to obey such an order would mean court martial and a firing squad, while after surrender the fact of having obeyed the order and committed a war crime could send you to the gallows. Hess is second from left in the first row of defendants in the dock.

commander who, after 3000 Persians had escaped him at Plateia, found 260 000 more who wished to surrender. If he had accepted their surrender, how would he have fed them?

In the campaigns of Charles XII of Sweden, 1800 years later, a company of men 300 strong needed ten four-horse waggons to carry only their provisions, so that to have supplied the Greek force of 33 000 and the 260 000 Persians who wished to surrender would have required between 9000 and 10 000 waggons (the figures in Greek sources are often inflated). This was logistically impossible, apart from the fact that the whole of Greece could scarcely have absorbed such a sudden increase in the slave population, while to have disarmed and released such a horde could have been a recipe for disaster. Slaughter was the chosen solution.

There is an essential difference between a refusal to accept surrender and the slaughter of prisoners whose surrender has already been accepted, as in the Katyn massacre of World War II. The latter is a War Crime, though when the perpetrator is one of the victors as in the case of Katyn, he cannot be brought to book for the crime.

The idea that laying down arms constitutes an offer of peace, that on which all the rules and regulations governing the treatment of prisoners of war are based, is itself based on the assumption that surrender is final, a

cessation of all hostilities on either side. When individuals, even in large numbers, have surrendered or been captured and the war goes on, their surrender is today little more than a request for a breathing-space, for the soldiers surrendering are probably duty bound to continue the struggle.

On July 3, 1863 the US War Department issued Order No 207 which made it clear that the duty of a US soldier captured by the other side was to escape. 'It was his duty to rejoin his own side as soon as the opportunity presented itself.' Thus the US soldier had not made any offer of peace, nor had he ceased hostilities. He was on the lookout for an opportunity to escape and rejoin his own side to resume the fight. In World War I it was accepted in most armies that this, too, was the duty at least of officers. The same applied in World War II. In 1953, General Dwight D Eisenhower issued Executive Order 10631 — Code of Conduct for Members of the United States Armed Forces — according to which the members of the armed forces effectively undertook, (a) never to surrender of their own free will, and (b) if captured to continue to resist by all means available; to make every effort to escape and to aid others to escape. Thus the American serviceman in captivity can scarcely be considered to have made an offer of peace.

In today's armies, the French soldier, whether officer or of other rank, who becomes a prisoner of war is duty bound to escape and to aid his companions to do likewise. 'Le devoir du prisonnier militaire est d'échapper à la captivité, de resister aux pressions et de *chercher à reprendre le combat* (Authors' italics)'. The Germans no longer give any instructions about this eventuality and neither do the Swedes.

Obviously, though some of today's soldiers who may become prisoners of war may capitulate and surrender completely, the majority must be considered as continuing to fight in one way or another. This they would do by trying to escape and rejoin their own side, by making a nuisance of themselves so that the maximum number of the enemy has to be employed guarding them, and, in the case of other ranks, by sabotaging the work which they are given to do. How can such men really have a status other than that of combatant?

One wonders what lawyers would make of Sidney Stewart's killing of the Japanese soldier who was robbing him and the other US soldiers in World War II of their watches, pens and whatever took his fancy. Sidney Stewart had fastened to his belt a first-aid pouch which contained, amongst other things, a good supply of sodium amytal tablets. The Japanese, thinking they were sweets or concentrated food, asked if they were 'good'. Stewart replied that they were and watched him pour a number into the palm of his hand and swallow what was well in excess of a lethal dose. Now, was Stewart continuing to fight although he had surrendered? Did he in effect kill an enemy in the course of war or in fact murder him?

THE FUTILITY OF BRAINWASHING

Another form of continued combat, though in this case on the part of the detaining power, is that of indoctrination, re-education or brainwashing. Experience has shown that as far as political opinion goes, most ordinary people are 'antis' rather than 'pros' and are seldom prepared to go to the wall for any particular school of thought. As many US soldiers captured in Vietnam explained on their return home, all politics are 'crap': there is Communist/Marxist crap, there is Capitalist crap, etc, but it is all crap and they could see little reason why one should not pay lip service to either one of them, if by doing so life was made more tolerable, or repatriation brought nearer.

The fact is that of the white troops captured by the Koreans and Chinese in Vietnam, most of whom were subjected to some form of cruel re-education grandiosely called brainwashing, only 22 elected not to return home to the capitalist world, while of Chinese/Koreans captured by the UNO forces 14 325 refused to be repatriated. One cannot believe that this difference was solely due to the persuasiveness of capitalist theory, but rather to the quality of the Americans' equipment (watches, pens, radios, etc) and the attraction of what the POWs saw of the capitalist way of life. There are few roads to Damascus and few Pauls. Those who do see the light are fanatics and when one has such a strong belief, neither reason nor argument enter into it: genuine faith is inviolable and, as the records of the Inquisition show, it is really a waste of time and effort to try and change it.

Another example of surrendered prisoners continuing to resist is Koje island, where the Korean communist POWs organized themselves and armed themselves to resist the UNO guards, and execute all who expressed a wish not to be repatriated. Those inspired by this kind of fanaticism were — in the words of the 57th Report of the UN Command for 1–5 November, 1952 — to be regarded 'not as a passive human being in need of care and protection until he could be returned to his home, but as still an active soldier determined to fight on in whatever way his leader dictated.' This was the first time that POWs en masse had remained combatants and carried out orders smuggled through to them from the enemy high command. In other words though there may have been a capture, there had been no surrender.

This, too, was the first war in which POWs had been granted the right not to be repatriated, if they did not wish to go home. Not that this wish was then new, for many of the former Red Army soldiers (eg, Ukrainians) who had been persuaded or encouraged to don German uniforms and were subsequently captured by the Allies had no wish to return to life beneath the yoke of their people's oppressors. But the Allies had already promised Stalin to return all 'Russians' who fell into Allied hands, and the Soviets insisted that they keep their promise. It was not that the Soviets were concerned for the men's welfare, far from it. It was, to quote Gerald Reitlinger, 'a concern lest ignorant and bewildered men, who had turned traitor even if only to avoid a slow death from hunger, should again escape punishment for not having died.'

The height of this bewilderment must surely have been the case of two men in German uniform captured by the Polish troops in Normandy in 1944. Although the Poles could muster most European languages and many of those of the Soviet Union, no one could understand what these two said and it was obvious that they were unable to understand what was said to them. In the end it transpired that they were Chinese herdsmen, whose herd had strayed across the frontier into Soviet territory. They had been captured, put into Russian uniform and sent to fight on the Eastern Front, where they had survived by imitating others: lying down when they lay down, getting up when they got up, running forwards or backwards as they did. Then they had been captured by the Germans and put into German uniform and the whole process had been repeated. When captured by the Poles the two Chinese men were still in complete ignorance of who was fighting whom and why. They were lucky: they were repatriated.

The Geneva Convention of 1929 had laid it down that repatriation of prisoners should be carried out as soon as possible after the declaration of peace — it not having occurred to anyone then that wars could end without a proper peace being concluded. Since a long interval may (and now normally does) exist between the declaration of an armistice and the signing of a peace treaty, this part of the convention was amended in 1949. Article 118 of the 1949 Geneva Convention now categorically states that prisoners shall be released and repatriated without delay after the cessation of active hostilities.

But what are 'active hostilities'? No military commander on the winning side would in common sense release his prisoners while there was still a fear in his mind that an armistice might be broken, or that there was a likelihood of it being disregarded by fanatical groups determined to hold out suicidally in areas difficult of access, as was intended in the German Werewolf plan in 1945.

Article 118, however, assumes that all prisoners want to be repatriated, yet in modern times, many whose country of origin is a dictatorship or has recently been 'liberated' by a foreign power, have had no wish to go back home. This is especially true when the fact of their having surrendered is in their rulers' eyes a capital offence and will probably earn them a bullet when they get 'home'. It was not until the Korean War, at the end of which the United Nations Command accepted that Korean or Chinese prisoners were not to be repatriated against their wishes, that there was this choice. This would have saved the lives of the many thousand Ukrainian and other POWs forcibly repatriated by the British and others at the end of World War II.

Not to have done so would have involved the detaining powers in considerable problems, absorbing POWs into their own communities or finding homes for them elsewhere.

TALES OF POW DISCIPLINE

In international law, the soldier who surrenders or is captured remains a member of his own armed forces and is subject to their military discipline, as well as to the rules for conduct of the camp laid down by the detaining power. In camps for officers, the senior officer of each country represented there is responsible for internal discipline among the officers to the camp commandant. He has, however, no legal power of enforcement, so the members of each force voluntarily maintain their own discipline as a matter of convenience and expediency. In a camp of British POWs, for example, there could be no legality for the trial and execution of a prisoner, such as that of the Luftwaffe officer by his fellow Germans in the British TV serial *The Secret Army*.

The facts on which this episode is based are almost as bizarre as the scene depicted. There were two executions, not of officers, but naval deserters: corporal/radio operator Bruno Dorfer; and coastguard Rainer Beck (the one aged 20, the other 28). Both had deserted and gone into hiding in Amsterdam. After the surrender of the Germans there, the two gave themselves up to the Canadian Army authorities, who put them in a camp for SS and SD people, (ie, those held as probable war criminals). Disliking their associates, the two sailors escaped from the camp and, for some reason never explained, went back to Beck's old coastguard unit, then in custody in a camp set up in the Ford car assembly plant on the Nordzee Canal just outside Amsterdam. The German camp commander Alexander Stein refused to accept them because they were deserters, until ordered to do so by the Canadians. What then happened is far from clear. One side maintains that the Germans asked to be allowed to court-martial the two and were given permission to do so; the Germans maintain that the Canadians ordered them to court-martial the two deserters. Any way, court-martialled they were and the death sentence was pronounced and an execution order duly signed by the Camp Commander. However, under German naval law, Stein had no authority to sign an order that required the signature of an admiral, and the only one able to have signed it at that time was Admiral Rudolf Stange, who was then in England. The Germans said that they never for a moment envisaged the sentence being carried out, but that the Canadians insisted they proceed with it and supplied the rifles and ammunition and transport to a place of execution, where the two were duly shot on May 13, 1945, eight days after the surrender of the German troops in the Netherlands. A Canadian officer was apparently present at the execution.

There are grounds for saying that this was a legal execution of two men justly sentenced for desertion. There are also grounds for saying that it was downright murder: hostilities had ceased, the Germans had surrendered, so the war was over and peace time rules should have applied.

Another tale of POW discipline has been told by Private Reginald Bellamy of the Machine Gun Corps, who was in a camp where the inmates became so hungry that stealing bread became common; so common, indeed, that people slept with their bread under their heads and by day carried it about with them, wherever they went. An Englishman was caught in the act of stealing bread and his fellow prisoners (ORs and NCOs) gave him the choice of being tried by court-martial of his peers (which would have ranked as a kangaroo court) or of being reported to the Germans. The poor man elected to be court-martialled. However, when he was sentenced to run the gauntlet and found himself facing an avenue of grim-faced men armed with wetted, knotted towels, his courage failed him and he elected to be handed over to the Germans instead. They subjected him to a more subtle punishment: he was deprived of his rations for 24 hours and had to spend the whole of one afternoon standing against a pole facing a loaf of bread on the ground a short distance away. He was not tied to the pole, but a rifle and bayonet was in the immediate offing to be used should he try to snatch the bread.

WHEN POWS ARE A LAW UNTO THEMSELVES

There are plenty of cases of fanatical POWs taking arbitrary, illegal action against their fellows, whom they had considered guilty of betraying their particular ideology (Nazism, Communism, etc). The North Koreans and Chinese were prime offenders here and the Nazis in American camps during World War II were guilty of intimidation, beatings, forced suicide and murder. One particularly grim example is that of Corporal Johann Kunze of Camp Tonkawa in Oklahoma. He was brought before a kangaroo court of 200 POWs, accused of passing to US officials information about the port of Hamburg that could have been useful in planning bombing raids. Such an offence might, indeed, have been treason were it not for the fact that the information was widely available having been printed in a number of American magazines. Kunze was beaten to death with clubs and broken milk bottles. Five sergeants of the Afrika Corps were then arrested by the US authorities and tried for murder by a US court-martial. Found guilty, they were hanged. At this, as at other such trials, a representative of the protecting power, in this case Switzerland, was always present.

Another case is that of a U-boat crewman, Werner Drechsler. His submarine, U-118, was sunk and the crew rescued and captured by the US Navy. Dreschler then changed sides and cooperated with US Naval Intelligence, even to the extent of adopting the identity of a petty officer and associating as a stool-pigeon with other naval prisoners in a camp at Fort Meade. Then, by mistake, he was transferred to a camp in Arizona, which contained a lot of U-boat crewmen, including some from his old ship, U-118. He was quickly recognized and within a few hours of his arrival was found hanging from a rafter. For this 'murder' seven German submariners were hanged. If Dreschler had been an officer and tried by court-martial instead of by a kangaroo court, would his execution have been legal and his excutioners gone scot free?

Further cases occurred in Britain during World War II, one of the worst perhaps being that of Wolfgang Rostberg. He had been implicated in a crack-brained escape plot which involved simultaneous breakouts from camps at Sheffield and Marchant in Wiltshire, the escapers seizing lorries while Christmas festivities were in full swing. When the two groups had linked up, they were to seize a radio station and send a message to Bremen asking for warships to be sent to somewhere on the east coast to pick them up. Fortunately the German navy never had to make the attempt, as the plot was discovered in advance, the ring-leaders being sent to the camp for confirmed Nazis at Comrie. Rostberg, a fluent English speaker, was among them. At Comrie he was suspected of not being as Nazi as his comrades and one night his diary was stolen and his doubts about Hitler were read out to his fellow prisoners. He was brought before a mock court-martial, found guilty of treason and hanged in the camp wash-house. Rough justice, perhaps, but if he had been an officer and tried by his peers, it would have been legal in international law.

How the POW's status has evolved over the ages

Up to the mid-seventeenth century a prisoner of war was the chattel of his captor. Many were sold into slavery or ransomed; some were exchanged; many were killed because nobody wanted them as was the case in North Korea in the mid-twentieth century.

After the seventeenth century it was generally agreed that the POW was in the power of the state that captured him, not of the individual captor, so that the responsibility for his treatment rested with the state, thus paving the way for the international conventions of the nineteenth and twentieth centuries.

Although the prisoner of antiquity had no rights as far as the enemy was concerned, many had rights at home. The Assyrian Code of Hammurabi (2000 BC) assured the POW of help from home in paying his ransom if he was captured and laid it down that his wife must not leave him while provisions lasted in their home, and should in any event go back to him on his return.

'Too much confidence must not be placed in regulations concerning the conduct of war. Military necessity, the heat of action, the violence of the feelings which come into play will always at times defeat the most skillfully combined rules diplomacy can devise.' — *Encyclopaedia Britannica*, 11th edition.

BC 400 Plato propounds the view that the soldier who gives up fighting deserves whatever happens to him as a prisoner.

1179 AD The Third Lateran Council decrees that Christian POWs should no longer be sold as slaves, though no one appears to have paid much attention to the edict.

1100–1800 In the many wars against the forces of Islam Christian prisoners are able to save their necks by selling their souls and embracing Islam.

1637 French writer Gabriel Naudé puts forward the suggestion that those who surrender but cannot pay a ransom need not be put to death.

1758 French jurist Vattel praises the generous treatment of POWs by both the French and English.

1780 France and England make the last cartel governing rates for ransoming of all ranks. This was little used as most prefered to wait for exchange and save their money.

1785 Prussia and the United States sign a Treaty of Friendship (never invoked) which contained many of the provisions of the later Hague Regulations, such as that prisoners should not be confined in civil convict prisons nor fettered, and that they were to have rations on the same scale as the captor's own troops.

1863 The American 'Instructions to Armed Forces' Art 60, repeats the traditional view that in an emergency a commander is at liberty to kill his prisoners.

1899 Hague Convention issues

Executions in Korea.

regulations governing the conduct of war, but leaves the awkward question of the prisoner of war to be decided eight years later.

1907 Hague Regulations governing treatment of the POW provide the first international rules generally accepted and acted upon, including the prohibition of declaring that no quarter will be given. These were the regulations in force during World War I.

1920 International Law Association recommends that laying down of arms be recognized as 'an offer of peace'.

1929 Geneva Convention amplifies and amends Hague Regulations.

1945 International acceptance through War Crimes Trials of concept of war crimes and the fact that he was obeying orders does not exonerate a soldier who commits an atrocity.

1946 Thousands of Ukrainian and other Soviet citizens forcibly repatriated by the Western Allies to Russia and their death.

1949 Amendments to the Geneva Convention signed by a number of states.

1952 The United Nations Command recognizes that a POW can still be 'an active soldier determined to fight on', implying that surrender need not necessarily be an offer of peace. UN also recognized that POWs can have the right *not* to be repatriated, if they do not wish to go home.

1953 US Order 207 restates the position that a US soldier taken prisoner is duty bound to try to escape.

CHAPTER 3

SURRENDER AND CAPTURE

Unlikely as it may seem in the midst of this mêlée, capture in battle has its own particular code of practice.

Surrender may be the decision of an isolated individual or small group of individuals, who for a number of reasons find themselves physically unable to continue fighting, or else hopelessly outnumbered. Exactly when this point has been reached is a question of individual judgement, and the history of war abounds in examples of small groups deciding to surrender and then being shot down by their fellows who do not wish to surrender. Where greater numbers are concerned (anything up to a whole army) the decision to surrender will be taken by the commander and the order passed down the usual chain of command. The reasons for surrender will be the same in both cases: lack of supplies (food, water, ammunition) and no prospect of replenishing them; physical exhaustion caused by a lengthy battle; lack of sleep (that great enemy of discipline and morale) and loss of incentive. Another common cause of surrender has been bad intelligence, which has left the forces surrendering ignorant of the true strength or weakness of the enemy. On paper, certain famous surrenders have been quite unnecessary: that of the Swedes after Poltawa is an example.

The armies of Charles XII (1682-1718) were as successful as those of Napoleon a hundred years later. The Swedes' reputation was tremendous and they had come to consider themselves well-nigh invincible. Then in 1708 things began to go wrong. At first it was only minor set-backs but sufficient to sow the seeds of doubt. At the end of April 1709 the Swedish army was besieging Poltawa — an objective not of prime importance — situated between two tributaries of the Dnieper, the Worskla and the lesser Psiol. The arrival of Russian reinforcements precipitated an engagement in which the Russians came off best. Early in the engagement the Swedish king was wounded in the left foot. The wound caused him to faint when dismounting some hours later. His foot was then operated on and shortly after-

A North Korean Army captive being searched by men of the 3rd Engineers 187 Abn Regiment on February 4, 1951.

wards gangrene set in, forcing the king to take to a litter. He twice left the litter and mounted his horse, so that the troops would see him and take heart; this, however, re-opened the wound, causing considerable loss of blood and effectively depriving the king of the ability to lead and command.

This battle cost the Swedes less than 10 000 men, leaving them with as many still fit to fight, and these were re-grouped just to the south at Perevolotnja. Here a Russian force of only 4000 infantry with some guns and 400 irregular horse attacked them. The Russians were almost as exhausted as the Swedes and inferior in training and experience — yet the Swedes surrendered after very little fighting. Their surrender was inevitable. The king, the troops' inspiration, was so ill that his presence and the possibility of his capture had been thought a liability, so he had been persuaded to leave the army and make for safety in Turkey. This, of course, was known.

The Swedish generals then had unwisely called the regimental commanders to a council of war at which they were asked to find out whether their men, who had had little or no sleep for five days, were prepared to continue fighting. Just to ask such a question suggested that the generals thought the outcome doubtful. The troops themselves had for some time had a nagging feeling that the king's luck had changed and that things were no longer going their way. They knew that the king was no longer with his army or in charge; that a small regiment of Tartars had melted away during the night; and now here were their officers, as weary and dispirited as they, asking them if they wished to continue fighting! Some began slipping across the river: they had had enough and were heading for home even though home was a thousand miles away. The officers were unable or unwilling to stop them. It was the end.

Yet, on paper, there was no reason whatever for the Swedes to have surrendered. That they did so, so surprised the Russian commander that he admitted as much. There are other cases where a few hours sleep might well have changed the course of history, and many more when better intelligence would have prevented surrender, if not the final outcome. The conflict in the Falklands in 1982 is a case in point.

In antiquity, battle for the foot soldier meant hand-to-hand fighting with sword and spear, even actual wrestling, in which all soldiers were trained. What it was like for the mounted knight of later centuries is vividly described by Joinville in his account of the battle of Mansourah (1250) during the Fourth Crusade.

'As we were pursuing them through the camp I caught sight of a Saracen on the point of mounting his horse; one of his knights was holding the bridle. At that moment he had both his hands on the saddle to pull himself up, I gave him a thrust with my lance just under the armpit and struck him dead. On seeing this, his knight left his lord and the horse, and thrusting his lance at me as I passed, caught me between the shoulders, pinning me down to the neck of my horse in such a way that I could not draw my sword at my belt. I therefore had to draw the sword attached to my horse. When he saw me with my sword drawn he withdrew his lance and left me . . . As I was coming back, the Turks thrust at me with their lances. Under the weight of their attack my horse was brought to its knees, and I went flying over its ears. I got up as soon as ever I could, with my shield at my neck and sword in hand . . . One of my knights advised our drawing back towards a ruined house . . . As we were going there, some on foot and some on horseback, a great body of Turks came rushing at us, bearing me to the ground and riding over my body, so that my shield went flying from my neck . . .'

Houses built on the banks of the River Intis at Tobolsk for some of the Swedes captured at Poltava.

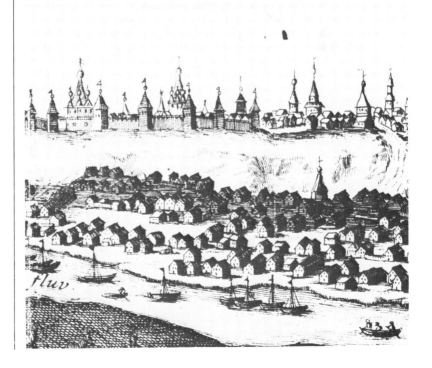

The white flag is universally recognized as a symbol of surrender. Here a column of Germans who have just surrendered, are being marched to the collecting point with hands raised, because they have not yet been searched, their NCO still holding the white flag that announced that they were giving up. The roadside trees provide mute evidence of the fierceness of the battle.

During this incident, Huhues d'Écot received three wounds in the face from a lance, and so did Raoul de Wanou, while Frédéric de Loupey had a lance-thrust between his shoulders, which made so large a hole that the blood poured from his body as if from the bung-hole of a barrel. A blow from one of the enemy's swords landed in the middle of Erard de Silverey's face, cutting through his nose so that it was left dangling over his lips . . . It was, I can assure you, a truly noble passage of arms, for no one there drew either bow or crossbow; it was a battle of maces against swords between the Turks and our people, with both sides inextricably entangled.'

When he realized that he had to give up, the soldier of antiquity dropped to his knees, or squatted on the ground, and clasped his opponent's knees, right hand or even his chin, in a gesture of supplication. If not engaged hand-to-hand, he put his hands up — the Spartans did this at Sphacteria and the Macedonians at Cynoscephalos. Another way was to raise your arms with the little fingers extended — as the Libyans did when surrendering to the ancient Egyptians; or, if carrying a sword, they held the sword upright in the right hand and extended the left arm horizontally, palm down. Much later, a white flag became common usage. But if you gave up in the middle of a battle, what could you expect but the coup-de-grâce? Your captor had to go on fighting until the outcome had been decided, and could hardly be expected to pause long enough to take you to the rear and secure you there.

It was only at the end of a battle, when your captor's side had already won, that you could expect him to have the time to take you prisoner. Even so, there have been occasions when, though the outcome seemed decided, the enemy has regrouped and attacked again, or as in the case of Agincourt in 1415, is presumed to be doing so. When that happened, prisoners already taken could not be left unguarded and unfettered, in case they took what

Russians surrendering to the Austrians on the Eastern Front in World War I. The rifles planted, muzzle down, in the parapet are an additional sign of surrender.

arms were lying about and attacked their captors from the rear: they had to be killed. At Agincourt, the order to do this was not obeyed, because the soldiers were reluctant to destroy their chance of collecting a ransom, and the king had to detail an esquire and 200 archers to do the grisly job for them.

It is impossible to imagine what it felt like to surrender in such circumstances, knowing that your chances of survival were slim. Those who surrendered in this way, were probably so exhausted at the time of surrender that they no longer cared what happened to them, as long as they did not have to go on struggling.

Those who surrendered to the Romans, if their lives were spared, had to pass beneath the yoke (three spears, two set upright in the ground, the third lying horizontally between them) symbolizing their new status as a slave, before being herded off into captivity and whatever fate awaited them there. The word 'slavery' has an ugly sound to twentieth-century ears and with every justification, considering the conditions of slavery under the Soviets and Nazis, but in antiquity things could be very different. An efficient slave was valuable and his owner, if a sensible and practical person, looked after him, supplying his needs and some (if not all) of his wants. If a slave had a particular skill — as a cook, scribe, chariot-driver, gladiator, etc — he was allowed to practise it and earned money by doing so, so that he was really no worse off than his modern counterpart, say the footballer who is bought and sold by the clubs for which he plays.

But surrender did not always mean captivity, let alone slavery. When the knights of St John surrendered Rhodes to Suleyman, he gave them the full honours of war; and when Saladin finally captured Jerusalem (1187) his treatment of the vanquished was exemplary. Steven Runciman has described it thus in his *A History of the Crusades*:

'It was arranged that for 30,000 dinars seven thousand should be freed.

On Balian's orders the garrison laid down its arms; and on Friday 2 October, Saladin entered Jerusalem. It was the 27th day of Rajab, the anniversary of the day when the Prophet in his sleep had visited Jerusalem and had been wafted thence to Heaven.

The victors were correct and humane. Where the Franks, years before, had waded through the blood of their victims, not a building now was looted, not a person injured. By Saladin's orders guards patrolled the streets and the gates, preventing any outrage on the Christians . . . Soon two streams of Christians poured out through the gates, the one of those whose ransoms (10 dinars a man, 5 a woman and 1 a child) had been paid by themselves or by Balian's efforts, the other of those who could afford no ransom and were going into captivity. So pathetic was the sight that al-Adil turned to his brother and asked for a thousand of them as a reward for his services. They were granted to him and he at once set them free. The Patriarch Heraclius, delighted to find so cheap a way of doing good, then asked that he might have some slaves to liberate. He was granted seven hundred, and five hundred more were given to Balian. Then Saladin himself announced that he would liberate every aged man and woman. When the Frankish ladies who had ransomed themselves came in tears to ask him where they should go, for their husbands or fathers were slain or captive, he answered by promising to release every captive husband, and to the widows and orphans he gave gifts from his own treasury, to each according to her estate. His mercy and kindness were in strange contrast to the deeds of the Christian conquerors of the First Crusade.'

A soldier does not necessarily have to surrender to become a prisoner of war;

A German surrendering as he runs from a disabled armoured car that might explode at any moment. Had he jumped out without his hands in surrender position, it would have invited a burst from an automatic rifle.

he can be captured, physically thrown to the ground, as was often the case with knights in armour, or be incapacitated by wounds; the fate of Count Beniowski and countless others. Beniowski, a member of the Confederacy of Bar, and his regiment of cavalry engaged the Russians near Tarnopol in 1768. The Count had received two sabre wounds in previous engagements and now, his regiment having been surprised by Cossacks in the village of Szuka, a shot from a cannon 'loaded with old iron and other destructive rubbish' knocked the Count out of his saddle and he was captured.

There were many bizarre ways to be captured. During World War I for example, Robert Neubau, armed with a bicycle and a revolver, was acting as Company runner and liaison man when the Germans made contact with the retreating French in a small town on the Oise. In the course of his duties Neubau found himself at Regimental HQ, where the General ordered him to bicycle ahead and see if he could discover what the French were doing. He had scarcely pedalled half a mile when as he was passing some houses, a man rushed out and aimed a blow at him with the butt of his rifle. The blow missed the rider, but struck and buckled the rear wheel, so that Neubau was thrown to the ground and willing hands seized him and made him captive!

It was by no means uncommon in World War I for a patrol to go out by night across No-Man's-Land to try and seize a couple of prisoners in the enemy's trenches and drag or frog-march them back to their own lines for identification of their unit and further interrogation. In World War II, the long-distance patrols that the Finns operated, anything up to 100 miles into Russian territory, not infrequently took a middle-ranking prisoner and brought him back through miles of enemy land and two front lines to be interrogated at Finnish Army HQ. There is something ignominious in being captured by brute force in this way, especially when snugly asleep in your bed, as happened to at least one of these Russians, which is why one British major of the author's acquaintance always slept in his battle-dress trousers!

Surrender is often a confession of failure, but it too can have its comical side. In 1916, Duncan Grinnell-Milne's engine refused to function while the 'plane he was flying with his observer, Strong, was still over enemy territory. They lost height rapidly and soon the only thing to be done was to attempt a landing.

' . . . turning into the wind, I landed in a ploughed field. Strong and I immediately jumped out and held a hurried consultation. Neither of us really believed that we had crossed the trenches, although we tried to pretend to each other that there was nothing to worry about. I asked Strong to go to the edge of the field and look over the brow of the hill, towards the village, to see if anyone was coming. He had gone barely a few seconds, when I heard a yell: turning round I saw him running back shouting that the Germans were coming. The last glimpse of hope disappeared and there was only one more thing to be done. I went round to the front of the machine, pulled off a rubber connection and set fire to the petrol. By the time the foremost Germans breasted the hill, there was little to be seen of our unfortunate craft but a cloud of smoke and a blaze of flame . . . It was no use running away; the Germans were coming up on two sides, about 200 strong, and there was no cover in which we could take refuge. And so, standing by our burning machine we awaited their arrival.

'They came up at the double, headed by a NCO on a horse. All at once, when they were still some ten yards away, they came to a full stop, checked by a series of loud explosions which suddenly occurred in the

Overleaf: American POWs on Corregidor are herded down to boats for transfer to Bataan while Japanese infantry move up to take over Corregidor's fortress, May 7, 1942. As one captive has been allowed to retain his cigarette, things could presumably be worse.

aeroplane: the ammunition of the machine-gun had evidently reached boiling-point and was beginning to go off. The effect on the Germans was quite extraordinary. Half their number threw themselves flat on their faces, while the remainder took refuge in flight. On those who were lying down I tried a few phrases of my choicest German, inform-ing them that we quite harmless and would like to surrender . . . It was a strange position to be in: we begged to be allowed to surrender and our enemies either lay flat on the ground in front of us or ran away . . . presently, when our ammunition had burned itself out, they plucked up courage and started to return . . . Then some German flying officers arrived and introduced themselves with much bowing and saluting, as if war had never existed.'

PRACTICAL
PROBLEMS

That was how two men surrendered, but what about a whole garrison or army? The British officers attached as observers to the Japanese forces besieging Port Arthur during the Russo-Japanese War (1904–05) wrote an account of its capitulation. This was a premature surrender initiated without the knowledge of his fellow commanders by General Stessel, who on his own initiative sent an emissary to General Nogi, the Japanese commander, at the same time informing the admiral commanding the Russian fleet there that he had only one night in which to destroy his ships and stores.

Throughout the siege there was only one instance when the white flag was used as an indication of the desire to surrender, which was during the attack on Fort Sung-Shu, when, according to the *Official History of the Russo-Japanese War*:

'. . . The survivors of the garrison, sheltering in the gorge casemates (recesses in the walls), thus found themselves cut off from all hope of escape; but they were in telephonic communication with the staff of the fortress, and received instruction to the effect that any man who so wished might endeavour to escape, and that those who did not care to make the attempt might surrender. The telephone was then destroyed in order to prevent the Japanese from tapping the wire. Practically there was no choice, for there was absolutely no chance of escape, and about 11.30 a.m. a white flag was thrust up from the windows . . . For some time no notice was taken of the signal, and the Japanese maintained a hot artillery duel with the batteries in the rear. At 1 p.m. the flag was lowered, but was raised again at 2 o'clock, and a few hours later, when the artillery fire slackened, two Russian officers and one hundred and sixty men were taken alive out of the ruins of the fort . . .'

As soon as the Japanese agreed to open negotiations firing died away on either side. The silence of the night was broken only by the sound of the explosions as the Russian fleet destroyed its ships. In the morning the repre-sentatives of both sides met in a village in No-Man's-Land. The Japanese presented a draft of their terms, written in English, and the Russians could do little though they did try to get the Japanese to agree that the garrison should not be made prisoners of war. The Japanese would not accept this.

What followed the final capitulation seems to be an extraordinary reversal of rôles. The annals of war are full of horrifying descriptions of towns being looted by the besieging army, the conqueror, but in the case of Port Arthur it was the other way round:

'As soon as the Russian troops heard the news (of the surrender) a large number of them flung their arms away and began to loot the town; the

Un-uniformed
Republican troops
surrending during the
Spanish Civil War.

Overleaf: Russians
captured by the Austrians
in World War I. The
problems presented by
the sudden capture of
such huge numbers can
be readily imagined.

streets were filled with drunken men, and many disgraceful scenes occurred before order was restored.'

By the evening of January 7, 1905 all the Russian prisoners of war had been taken over: 878 officers and 23 491 men, instead of the 10 000 the Japanese had been led to expect.

A comparable number were taken prisoner at Tannenberg nine years later, early in World War I. Lieutenant Herder of the 32nd Infantry Regiment of the German 1st Corps has described the end of the fighting:

'Eventually, they came towards us with a very large white flag, the Russian officers telling their men to throw away their arms, so we accepted the surrender. We took 20,000 prisoners . . . The hundreds of officers were rounded up in two farmhouses, while the men, desperately hungry, were put in fields where they had to stay for several days on muddy ground. It was a ghastly sight.'

When in World War I, General Townsend and his mixed force of British

and Indian troops were shut up in Kut-el-Amara and the relieving force was unable to break through the Turkish lines, surrender came almost as an anticlimax. It had been discussed for weeks, as supplies of food and ammunition dwindled, then one morning a small group of British officers left the beleaguered city and a few hours later a group of Turks arrived and Turkish sentries replaced the British. It was all over and 10 000 men were prisoners.

Ten times that number surrendered at Stalingrad in equally undramatic circumstances. The great German 6th Army consisting of some 300 000 men was encircled at Stalingrad on the Volga by an even greater number of Russians in 1944. When it became obvious that the Germans were not going to be able to break out — nor would Hitler entertain the idea that they should try — some supplies were flown in and men flown out in the returning 'planes, but such supplies were a tiny fraction and the troops were not only exhausted by weeks of fighting, but all but without food, ammunition or fuel to combat the cold. Of the 300 000 some 170 000 were killed in the fighting, about 30 000 were flown out and the remaining 100 000 eventually surrendered.

One might have expected some great show of chivalry, a spectacular meeting of Field-Marshalls, commanders of such huge numbers of men, a ceremonial breaking of swords, but instead General Roske sent his adjutant and an interpreter under a white flag to tell the Russians that his 'big chief' wished to talk with their 'big chief'. This message was conveyed to a 21-year-old lieutenant, Fedor Ilchenko, who told the Germans: 'I am the big chief here. Take me to your man!' Lieutenant Ilchenko was taken to General Roske, who had with him Field-Marshall Paulus' chief-of-staff, General Schmidt. Some hours later Paulus himself was taken to Russian 64th Army HQ and so on to Rokossovky's command post, but he had surrendered long before the two marshalls met.

An earlier surrender, one that did not have as great an impact on the course of the war as Stalingrad's but which was psychologically as important, was that of Warsaw to the invading German forces in 1939. The situation at the end was unusual: after 28 days the Polish defences were intact, the troops still had ammunition, and food was still coming into the city from the surrounding countryside through the German lines. But the Poles had no air force, no air defences, and the *Luftwaffe* was systematically destroying the city, above all its water and sewage works, thus creating an intolerable situation that forced capitulation. There was no water to put out the fires; no water to remove sewage; no water with which to cook food; no water to drink; no water to live. Halina Regulska went through it all. She noted in her diary:

> 'Suddenly from the distance an ominous growl. Another raid! Everyone made in haste to the shelters, dived into doorways. It was a whole squadron. Low, very low, scarcely above the rooftops, just above our heads. Why didn't they shoot at us, why didn't they drop bombs? We didn't even manage to see them, and so didn't know whose they were: German? Soviet? Polish? It was troubling. Excitedly people asked each other what it all meant . . .'

What it meant was this:

> 'Early this morning our delegation consisting of General Tadeusz Kutrzeba, Colonel Aleksander Praglowski and Captain Tadeusz Wojciechowski crossed the front and went to the German HQ. The German HQ agreed to a twenty-four hour truce, during which detailed

conditions for the surrender of the city and the disarming of the troops had to be worked out.'

It was to be a capitulation with honour. The troops were to lay down their arms and the civilian population be disarmed, before the Germans entered the city. No exact date for this entry was fixed, but it took place about October 1.

Water was the trump card. Without it, the besieged, however well-equipped otherwise, could not continue to resist. The capture of the McRitchie Reservoir in 1941 by the Japanese decided the fate of Singapore.

In mass surrenders the drama is never so intense, for the two sides are not now face to face. Though there may be a corporate numbness there is scarcely any personal element in it. When nearly a quarter of a million German and Italian troops suddenly surrendered at Tunis in May 1943 there was no sign of the numbness. To the British commander General Alexander, it 'was like Derby Day. Men, who a short time before had been fighting like tigers, now seemed transformed into a cheerful, docile crowd, resigned to the acceptance of their fate'. Indeed, as they waited to be taken into the cage on the Massicourt Road, a German band marched up, complete with instruments, and stood in a square, playing soothing Viennese music.

But what happens when a whole country surrenders, as France did in 1940? Then people's reactions differ widely: some feel betrayed by 'them', the politicians, generals, etc; some are just secretly grateful that they are not to be called upon to risk their lives, others are overjoyed at the fact that now their skins are safe, while others are so revolted by the sight of these latter dancing and leaping for joy and so ashamed at being told to surrender before they have done anything in defence of their country, that they refuse to obey the order. One unit that felt this way contained Francis Ambrière, author of *The Exiled*, who has described how they withdrew into the forest where their CO divided among them all the food they had and told them that now it was every man for himself: to try to get home, try to join the Free French through a neutral country, surrender or even have a go at the Boche as a one-man army. Francis Ambrière and some of his companions thought they would try to make their way to Switzerland through the Belfort Gap, but their enterprise was quickly nipped in the bud, for the Germans were already making a thorough search of the forest and surrounded them:

> '. . . three sub-machine-guns levelled in our direction persuaded us that the time had come to surrender. We had to go through the degrading performance of raising our hands, submitting to a cursory search and joining the long column which already contained several members of our unit.'

THE PSYCHOLOGY OF SURRENDER

During World War I it was still considered in a way dishonourable to be made a prisoner, for people had not yet accepted the notion that there was really nothing shameful in being outmanoeuvred or encircled and unable to fight your way out. In World War II most soldiers saw nothing shameful in being captured, though not all. One of these was a Parisian with whom Francis Ambrière struck up a friendship in the army, 'a proud nervous creature, who lacked patience and was unable to swallow his personal sense of shame', two months after his forced surrender he volunteered for work in the establishment of a Rhineland castle and there, using his employer's sporting gun, shot himself.

By the end of World War II no one on either side could feel that he had not done, or had not had time to do 'his bit', and people's individual surrenders were more pragmatic, like that of the Bavarian farmer who, in July 1944, found himself driving four horses harnessed to an ammunition waggon along a road in Normandy, when the British suddenly appeared ahead of him. Mindful of the load behind him, the farmer shouted 'Whoa!' to his horses, dropped the reins and put his hands up. About the same time in Picardy, an interpreter on the staff of a German Army Corps, found himself surrounded by a mixed unit of British, Free French and Resistance. Deciding that enough was enough, he climbed out of his foxhole and walked forward with his hands up. A quite elderly Frenchman, wearing a Resistance armlet, came up and asked what in the circumstances seems a peculiar question; 'Are you a Christian?' The German replied that he was: he was a Catholic. 'Ah', said the Frenchman, 'so am I; so we ought to be friends — but we aren't.' Then he offered the German a cigarette, helped him collect some of his belongings and took him to the assembly point.

Another form of surrender is internment, when an individual soldier or a group of soldiers, even a whole army, crosses the frontier into a neutral country. The neutral country may or may not accept belligerent troops who try to cross its frontiers. If it does, to preserve its neutrality it must disarm and guard them so that they do not take part in any further hostilites. The most remarkable instance in history was the internment in Switzerland during the Franco-Prussian war of an entire French army of 82 000 men and 10 000 horses. After the war France was presented with the bill for board and lodging, which amounted to over 11 million francs!

Compared with these enormous numbers, one individual instance may be quoted. In 1917 a Russian prisoner escaped from a camp in Schleswig and made for the Danish frontier. He was shot before reaching the frontier wire, but had suffcent strength to drag himself over it. He was hauled back by two German soldiers. The Danes protested and the Germans apologized: they would, they said, have gladly returned the Russian to neutral asylum in Denmark had he not, regrettably, died in the meantime.

Sailors traditionally dream of prize-money and the victorious soldier has long licked his lips at the thought of booty. The collection and exploitation of booty used to be well-organized and an internationally recognized perquisite of war, but now it is only the enemy's military equipment that is termed the spoils of war. However, the captured or surrendering soldier is likely to lose some or all of his personal valuables, strictly illegal though this may be. Most of the accounts of surrender or capture in the two world wars describe how the author had his watch, ring, fountain pen or some other personal article taken from him — sometimes before his weapons were taken — by a soldier whose eyes lit up at the sight of it. The Poles in 1939 were amused by the way the Russians put watch after watch on their arms like so many bangles, as did the Japanese. What is surprising is that the same thing is reported by German troops captured by the Americans towards the end of World War II. One writer recalls that in his unit they used to say that US did not mean United States, but Uhrensammler (watch collector). Spoils of war — to take an item or two for yourself is surely a very venial sin.

INTERROGATION—FACT AND FICTION

All prisoners of war are subject to interrogation on surrender. In the first place, they have to be listed and their names, numbers and units reported to their countries through the Protecting Power or the Red Cross. This information a prisoner is bound to give, but, according to international convention, he does not have to provide any more. Nonetheless, those thought

What thoughts are running through the minds of these German soldiers in Wolfheze, Holland as they surrender in front of civilian onlookers? Long considered an ignoble confession of failure, surrender was looked upon (with a few notable exceptions) as an altogether less shameful procedure during World War II, when great numbers of prisoners were being taken.

likely to be in possession of information of tactical or strategic value are often subjected to questioning by trained interrogators.

The soldier forcibly captured in enemy territory and brought back to his captor's lines in order to identify his unit may be induced to let slip items of information regarding units, locations etc that can be of immediate tactical use, but time quickly makes such information valueless.

Exaggerated claims have been made as to the successes of skilled interrogators. In *Intelligence is for Commanders* the authors claimed that POWs were the most profitable source of information in World War II. This seems a remarkable downgrading of Enigma, and, if true, suggests that more of warfare is guesswork than is commonly imagined! The authors of *Front-line Intelligence* state: 'Both German and Japanese in large numbers seemed to have no qualms whatever in giving away command post and observation post locations, gun positions, front lines, reserve assembly areas, artillery concentrations — in fact, anything and everything of value.' But by the time these men talked was their information any longer worth having? It must be

If this American pilot, shot down over Vietnam, has heard tales of the brainwashing that probably awaits him, he is perhaps wishing that he had not baled out but let himself be annihilated with his plane.

very tempting to give away information which you know to be no longer secret or of help to the enemy and so relieve the tedium of persistent questioning. A German interrogator of downed American flyers claims to have elicited all the information he wanted from all but a handful of the 500 American Air Force personnel he interrogated. But was that information of any value? Or anything he did not already know?

Farrago in his book *War of Wits* claims that Field Marshall Montgomery 'penetrated the most closely guarded secrets of his chief adversary, Marshall Erwin Rommel, when one of Rommel's top commanders, General Ritow von Thoma, fell into his hands'! Soldiers will talk shop as avidly as any professional. This may well provide an insight into their mentality — but will it really reveal their 'most closely guarded secrets'? It is impossible to strike a balance between the value of information obtained by interrogation and the cost of the effort of obtaining it. Those people sufficiently slow-witted to be tricked by a clever questioner are not likely to have knowledge of value to give away. The less intelligent are often promoted to put them out of harm's way, but they are not then employed on 'sensitive' work or where they are likely to be captured. The chatty, friendly interrogator can often elicit such facts as that the prisoner went to such-and-such a school, plays cricket, shoots and knows the Lake District, or has a passion for Brahms, but is that valuable?

The purpose of interrogation so far considered has been to obtain intelligence of value to the enemy, but the advent of Communism has seen a new form of interrogation the purpose of which is to undermine the prisoner's beliefs in his country and its political system, in his superiors, even in his God, so that he can be reprogrammed with his captor's beliefs and sent back to his own country in due course to act as evangelist or subversive agent. In the opinion of Colonel Perry, who provided Eugene Kinkhead with much of the information in his book *Why they collaborated*:

'The entire prisoner-indoctrination program of the Chinese was inspired, directed and in some ways assisted, by the Russians. Thousands of Austrians and Germans had been taken prisoner by the Russians in the Second World War, and were subjected to intensive questioning about their knowledge of life in America. Anything they might have gleaned from visiting America, from relatives living there, or from their own schooling was taken down. This information was passed along to the Chinese for use in dealing with Americans.

'The Russians are the masters, and, as a matter of fact, the originators, of the prisoner-of-war indoctrination process. It is an adaptation of the severe technique employed by them to extract cooperation and confessions from political prisoners, a phenomenon which was first noticed by the outside world during the Moscow Trials of the 1930's. Prisoner-of-war indoctrination started on the Eastern Front in World War II, nine years before the conflict in Korea. In October, 1941, the Red Army sent a directive to all its interrogators which stated in part, 'From the very moment of capture by the Red Army, and during the entire period of captivity, the enemy enlisted men and officers must be under continuous indoctrination by our political workers and interrogators.'

This continuing process of indoctrination is intended to turn the prisoner into a weapon to be used in the next war, whether cold or not, a mine to be planted in his own country furnished with a delayed-action fuse controlled by his erstwhile captor.

C H A P T E R   4

THE MARCH

Often the POW's worst sufferings have been endured in transit, on the way from the place of capture to his first camp. He will have had as a rule to walk much or even all of the way, sometimes chained as in a slave-gang. In antiquity, of course, a slave is what he had become.

The lands of the Middle East must have seen more POW traffic than any other part of the world. We do not know the route by which Tiglath-pileser and Nebuchadnezzar's commanders led or drove their captives to the lands round the Euphrates, but we do have an account of the sufferings of the French crusaders on their ignominious march in the opposite direction after their disastrous defeat at Nicopolis in 1396. It is retold by Barbara Tuchman in *A Distant Mirror*:

> 'The ordeal of the prisoners, many of them wounded, on their 350-mile march to Gallipoli was cruel. Stripped of clothing down to their shirts, in most cases without shoes, with hands tied, beaten and brutalized by their escorts, they followed on foot at their captor's heels over the mountain range and down onto the plain. To nobles equestrian almost from birth, the indignity of the barefoot trek was as great as the physical suffering. At Adrianople the Sultan paused for two weeks. The next stage took the march across the great, empty, treeless plain stretching, as if without horizon, towards the Hellespont. Not a bush nor shelter nor person was to be seen. The sun blazed down by day; when it set, the winds were chill and the October nights cold. In alien hands, uncared for and barely fed, crushed by defeat and fearful of the Sultan's intentions, the prisoners were in circumstances more dire than they had ever known . . .'

In those days, and for several centuries to come, prisoners were chained —

chains having been prepared in advance — and guarded by 'varlets, squires and almoners'. There was a practical reason for the use of chains: the modern equivalent of the 'varlet, squire and almoner' is armed with an automatic rifle which has an effective range of several hundred yards and so he can control a far larger number of prisoners than a man with a spear, sword or bow. Unfettered prisoners required a guard often more numerous than the captor could afford to detail for the purpose. It is true, however, that in some cases captives felt that for them the war was over, in which case they would scarcely need guarding at all.

An Austrian artist painted the Russian prisoners taken by Napoleon at Austerlitz in 1805 as they passed through Augsburg on their way to France. He depicts a seemingly endless column of shuffling men, reminiscent of the more dramatic photographs of World War I, guarded only by an occasional mounted dragoon and a few men on foot with bayonets fixed on their muskets and in their other hand a stout disciplinary cane. Many of these captives are bare-footed; some wear only foot-cloths; others have boots stuffed with the foot-grass of the far north. Two are drinking avidly, so thirst was perhaps their main problem; likely enough on a long march without any special provision to supply basic needs.

The distances prisoners have had to cover to reach their first place of detention have varied enormously. Caesar sent prisoners from Britain and Gaul to Rome, where they were displayed in his triumphs and then sold as slaves or slaughtered. Though the distances covered were sometimes enormous, there is no reason to suppose that the pace at which they travelled exceeded the 12 miles a day, far enough for defeated men, laid down by the Geneva and Hague Conventions; since that is the mean speed of draught oxen and presumably captives went along with the baggage train. The distances were certainly somewhat greater in seventeenth-century France, where the disposal of prisoners was swift and well organized. The stages into which their journeys were divided averaged between 15 and 22 miles.

BRUTALITY AND COMPASSION

The treatment of Christian prisoners by fellow Christians in modern times has varied greatly. There was the crude brutality endured by those captured by the forces of Charles VII at Pontoise in 1441, when they were sent to Paris tied like animals, roped to the tails of their captors' horses, half naked, famished, mostly without boots. On the other hand there was the superior treatment given to prisoners taken by the the French in their wars of the seventeenth century. Whenever a battle was won or a town captured and a sizeable number of prisoners taken, the French king sent a commissioner who took charge of the captives and arranged for them to be sent to parts of the country far enough away from the scene of fighting, or their own frontier, to prevent escape. The commissioner made detailed lists of the prisoners, taking down their names, surnames, rank and place of origin and arranged where they were to go and by what route. Usually he seems to have had them on their way with commendable despatch. For example those captured at Lens on August 20,1648 were first sent via Arras to Doullens, 50 miles away, where the Commissioner took them over on August 23. The first batch left Doullens on August 28 and they travelled, staging at Damart, Abbeville, Blangy, Neuchatel and Rocquemont to the outskirts of Rouen, where they had a day's rest. They then continued to Bourgtheroulde, Pont-Audemer, Blangy, Dives and Caen, where ten officers and 100 ORs were left; they continued to Bayeux which was allocated 15 officers and 90 ORs and here the others had a day's rest; then on to Saint-Lo, which had to take

Two medieval POWs, hands bound on their backs, stripped of their outer clothing and barefooted, being beaten by their guards as they are hounded into captivity. Such ill treatment was thought to hasten payment of the ransom they would have to pay.

six officers and 70 ORs, then to Carentan which was given 15 officers and 70 ORs, while the remaining 15 officers and 80 ORs continued to Coutances.

If it was possible, prisoners were conveyed by water, a man being sent ahead on foot to arrange for accommodation and supplies. Where they travelled by road, the escort was provided by the local authority from the municipal militia, the garde bourgeoise or, if necessary, from a scratch force of local volunteers. The local authorities also provided transport for the officers and baggage, and those who might be sick or disabled. Those too ill to move were given the best treatment available, and if they were gentry were lodged with an apothecary or such until they had recovered sufficiently to be able to continue on their way. Food and accommodation was provided locally and was paid for initially from local resources, the bill being sent to the government, which one hopes eventually paid it.

The daily allowance given for prisoners' subsistence during the same war was: for a captain, 20 sous; for a lieutenant 15 sous; for an ensign, cornet or quartermaster-sergeant ten sous; for a sergeant six sous; and for other ranks, four sous a day. Generals were not included, as they were normally exchanged swiftly.

A REMARKABLE ODYSSEY

Distance never seems to have been a consideration. Those paroled after the first battle of Tannenberg (1410) had to make their way to Cracow, a distance of 300 miles; Blaise of Montluc released after Pavia had to walk for 187 miles to reach the French frontier and then had another 250 miles to cover before reaching home. When the Russians invaded Prussia in 1760, they took prisoner among others, all the boys at the Cadet School in Berlin and sent them to Königsberg 375 miles away. This was no distance at all

An Austrian artist's depiction of Russian prisoners taken by Napoleon, January 1806.

compared with what faced the Swedish officers who were taken in the early years of the eighteenth century and after Poltawa in order to reach their places of detention in distant Siberia. Count Maurice Beniowski had to travel even further. A member of the Confederacy of Bar whom the Russians captured in 1769, near Tarnopol in Southern Poland, he was taken and thrown in chains, and put on bread and water. Shortly afterwards all POWs were ordered to be sent to Kiev, but Beniowski became so ill on the march that at Polone he had to be taken to hospital, where a French surgeon at last dressed his wounds. He and some others were allowed to lodge in the town while they recuperated, but then a new commandant was appointed who consigned them all to the prison dungeons, back on bread and water.

There were 80 of them. They were not allowed out for exercise or even to go to the latrine, so that within 20 days 35 of them had died, the bodies left lying in the filth among the living. Later the survivors were removed from the dungeon and attached to a column of some 700 others, all in chains, who were on the way to Kiev 312 miles away. The Russian officer in charge of the column pocketed half the allowance provided for the purchase of bread and other supplies, so that they were on very short rations. They slept out in the open, but that was no great hardship as it was July and high summer. Even so, only 148 reached Kiev 19 days later, the others either having died or, unable to go any further, had been abandoned in the forest. In Kiev they were put in casemates (chambers in the ramparts of fortresses), but after going down with a malignant fever Beniowski was allowed to lodge in the town until orders came for the POWs to set out for Kazan. Beniowski started with them but had to be left behind at Nezhin (after 80 miles) and he eventually joined a fresh batch of prisoners with whom he marched to Tula (300 miles away). Here Beniowski made his first escape, of which an account will be given later.

After his recapture in Petersburg Beniowski was sentenced to confinement in Kamchatka, to all intents and purposes at the other end of the world. His journey began in the depths of the Russian winter, on December 4. He was provided with a sheepskin coat, put in chains and made to mount a two-horse sleigh. They halted at noon for a meal which consisted of dry bread, and spent the night in a cottage. So it continued until they reached Volodomir on December 13. Here they were joined by four other prisoners and continued with them via Nizni Novgorod, Viattka, Saragut, and Tobolsk 2125 miles from Petersburg, which they reached on January 30. They left Tobolsk again on February 13, Beniowski at least having been provided with 50 roubles for subsistence, some brandy and a quantity of tobacco.

They were again two to a sleigh and so they reached Berenowsky, the escort on this leg of the journey being commanded by the son of a Swedish colonel who had been taken prisoner after Poltawa. Their way continued via Isirge to Juska, where the Tartars feasted them on mare's milk and horse flesh. The cold was intense and a blizzard immobilized them there for four days. Then, crossing the river, they reached Ahusca, Tara and Lukey through pretty well trackless forest and mountain. There was nothing but moss for the horses to eat and so each day's journey was comparatively short. On April 3 they camped beside the river Om, then crossed it and continued to the river Ob and then to Tomski. The country was now uninhabited forest and mountain. Their rations were reduced to half a pound of biscuit a day and each night they camped in the snow. On this leg the cold was such that they lost eight men of their Cossack escort and 12 horses.

They reached and crossed the Yenesei and continued across a vast plain of snow, in which they lost all their remaining horses and were reduced to eating birch bark. They continued on foot to the River Angara, and then to the Lena river, where they were embarked in birchbark canoes. They had a 'very commodious and agreeable' voyage to Jakutsk, which was reached on August 20. They left Jakutsk in sledges (drawn by what Beniowski says were elk, but which more probably were reindeer), crossed the Aldan in boats (the 'elk' swimming alongside), and on September 20 they reached the river Inna, where the cold was again so severe that two of the party froze to death. At a village on the river Yudoma they exchanged their reindeer sledges for dog sledges, which they had difficulty in learning to drive. Finally on October 16 they reached Ochotsk, where on November 22 they embarked in a 240-ton barque, the *St Peter and St Paul*, in which they sailed across the Sea of Ochotsk to their final destination, Kamchatka. They reached it on December 1, having covered well over 4700 miles in one year short of three days.

A hundred years later, during the Napoleonic Wars, when Britain took possession of all France's colonies, French POWs had to be sent back to Britain from places as distant as Pondicherry (in India) and the West Indies. Those captured by Abercrombie in Egypt were more fortunate, because they were so numerous and Britain was already accommodating so many POWs that the burden of that additional number could not be assumed, so they were all sent back to France in British ships.

When young Captain Charles Boothby of the Royal Engineers was wounded at the Battle of Talavera in 1809 he had to be left behind when the

British withdrew. His wounds were so severe that the British surgeons, who had stayed behind to look after the wounded, decided they must amputate his leg. The operation was performed without anaesthetic in the house where the very personable young Boothby was lodged. Boothby survived and was gradually restored to health. During his recovery unable to buy white bread and, anxious to get news to his parents in Ireland, he sent a diplomatic note to the French commandant invoking his help. This resulted in the commandant, General Séméllé, himself paying Boothby a visit, after which the prisoner was promised white bread and that letters to his parents would be sent under a white flag to the British lines, and from there to his home in Ireland.

Another example of modern chivalry was provided by General Mouravieff, who commanded the Russian forces besieging the fortress of Kars in Anatolia during the Crimean War (1854–1856). He was informed that, among intercepted letters and despatches for the garrison of Kars was a packet containing the Burma Medal awarded to Captain Thompson, a British officer attached to the Turkish garrison. Mouravieff had the package sent under a white flag to the lines at Kars, so that it could be safely delivered with his compliments and congratulations.

The siege of Kars provides a good illustration of the degree to which the

These prisoners captured in the course of the Spanish Civil War are at least fortunate in that they are bound with cord rather than the wire which some prisoners had to endure.

physical condition of those surrendering can affect the treatment they receive after surrender. The garrison of Kars did not surrender until the stores contained only one day's supply of rations, so meagre that on the day before the capitulation 230 men died of starvation. They were in fact all starving, for when the 18 000 survivors marched out a further 18 men fell dead while covering the relatively short distance to the Russian camp. What were the Russian quartermasters to do with that number of men in such a condition that, when given bread and soup in the Russian camp, 'even this simple fare was fatal to many of them, and they died of repletion in a few hours'?

An earlier example is that of the French captured during Napoleon's retreat from Moscow in 1812. We know that of the 30 000 French captured in Wilna, 25 000 died of typhus. Those in other cities were also near death; in Rjasan, for example, they all died within 48 hours of surrendering. French historians have concluded that in this case nature was the only executioner. Again and again it can be observed how much the treatment received depends on numbers. Large numbers present problems that are often insoluble even with the best will in the world; while where only a few are concerned, there is often no question of shortages or suffering, scarcely of inconvenience. Witness the journey into captivity of the British officers included in the surrender of Kars. On the first evening of their captivity they were 'entertained by the Russian general at his own quarters, in the most sumptuous style . . . The officers, after dinner, crowded round us, eager to learn whatever they could of the long defence, and insisted on our going to their tents with them to drink champagne . . . Next day, I amused myself by walking over the camp, chatting with many of the Russian officers, almost all of whom spoke French and German, and some of them English. They were kind and affable in the extreme.'

On November 30 the five Britishers, General Williams, his civilian secretary, Mr Churchill, Colonel Lake, Major Teesdale and Captain Thompson, and their servants set out for Tiflis, escorted by the Russian general's ADC. The Colonel's account of his journey which lasted until he finally reached Penza, 700 miles east of Moscow, on February 20, reads more like the diary of a package tour than of a prisoner of war's journey into captivity:

'*Yeni-Keni*: Invited to breakfast by Colonel Esackoff . . . *Vesi-Keni*: lodged in a hut built for the commanding officer, and, "after an excellent dinner and an ample supply of wine, turned in on our mattresses laid on the floor in a room." *Hadgi Veli Keni*: Breakfasted with a Prince. *Gumriy*: "a most comfortable house had been prepared for us . . . we were superbly treated . . . champagne sparkled in our glasses, and claret gurgled forth from the decanter with that gushing music so peculiar to the best of wines . . . Spent a delightful evening at the house of Princess Dondukoff." They left Gumri for Tiflis, the General and Colonel in a "large and luxurious britska drawn by six horses." (the general's servant being mounted on the box), the others in a somewhat smaller vehicle . . . "the rear brought up by two light postcarts filled with our wearing apparel, canteens and provisions." Some of the posting stations at which they had to stay were small and mean, but their Russian escort, Captain Bashmakoff, was "a jailer of the most delightful clemency, and who lavished the money of his Government on our comfort with laudable liberality." And so they reached Tiflis: "We were lodged in a magnificent house . . . that had been taken by the

Russian Government for our accommodation . . . We could each of us now enjoy a bedroom to himself and we had two large sitting rooms for general use." In Tiflis "we amused ourselves by going to the theatre, where our party very comfortably filled a box . . . The liberality of the Russian Government was boundless." Then they were ordered to go to Voronesh to await further instruction: "we were all supplied with fur coats, boots and caps of the most costly and comfortable kind . . . Our servants were also supplied with warm and useful articles." '

Bad weather and bad roads made the journey through the Caucasus difficult and uncomfortable, but once through the mountains, the diary takes up the same story:

'*Arden*: . . . we dined with him sumptuously and after dinner his wife played to us on the piano . . . *Stavropol*: . . . dined at the club, a small but very well arranged and comfortable institution . . . With the Russian officers who had so kindly placed it at our disposal we had a great deal of conversation. The 25th received an invitation to dine with General Koslovsky . . . in the evening we drank tea in the house of Madame Varpachoffsky . . . we were ungallant enough to leave this charming circle as early as nine, for the sake of going to the theatre — which was a dreadful disappointment. *Tichinski*: entertained with wine, biscuits, vodki by the village priest. The father of the Mayor, much affected at the idea of their being prisoners so far away from their homes, insisted on their going to his house, where they were "pressed to partake of caviar, fish, biscuits, wine and vodki. The Russians take no denial . . ." '*Tamboff*: Breakfast with the Governor (called to St Petersburg), dined with governor's wife and after dinner went to a soireé and dance at a private house. The following evening go to the theatre (the Governor's box) and on to supper at a private house. On the following Sunday dined at a private house which had its own orchestra of 30 performers. Finally, *Penza*: At our hotel we occupied three suites of rooms — not a bad cell for a wretched captive. Each suite consisted of a small entrance passage, a large airy sitting-room, and a small bedroom, well furnished, and very comfortable. Thompson occupied one suite, I another, and our two servants the third. (At this juncture Colonel Lake writes:) My diary at Penza is such a repetition of pleasant parties, kind attentions, and all that is agreeable to remember, that I fear I shall shock the minds of well-regulated people who probably think that a prisoner should have been consistently miserable . . .'

JOURNEYS INTO CONFINEMENT

When Robert Neubau was thrown off his bicycle and taken prisoner by the French in the early days of World War I, life in France was relatively normal and there was no difficulty in transporting him, a single prisoner, expeditiously and by train to a tented camp in Brittany 562 miles away. He travelled in comfort, though not, perhaps, as great comfort as Duncan Grinnell-Milne and his observer, who made the first leg of their journey into captivity in a railway carriage, with meals sent in from the dining-car at the escorting officer's expense.

Contrasting these with the journeys of Captain E O Mousley of the Indian Army, taken prisoner at Kut-el-Amara in 1916, one would think the two campaigns had taken place in different ages, not in the same war.

Captain Mousley had been wounded before the British surrender and so the first leg of his journey was in a river boat requisitioned to act as hospital ship. It was a journey of many stops, for the boat was continually running out of fuel and at each stop the Arabs came to within a yard of the boat dancing in ecstasy, gibing at the British and drawing their fingers across their throats to indicate what their fate ought to be. Enteric had been rife in Kut and every time the boat stopped, they had to bury the dead. Mousley describes how a man suddenly 'turned green and foamed at the mouth. His eyes became sightless and the most terrible moans conceivable came from his inner being, a wild horrible retching sort of vomiting groan. They died, one and all, with terrible suddeness.'

These conditions were not due to ill will on the part of the Turks, as another survivor of Kut has explained:

'When the Turks occupied Kut, they found themselves called upon to take charge of a large number of wounded, sick and starving soldiers and non-combatants with wholly inadequate arrangements for so doing; and the result was that many men of the garrison succumbed during the next two months to the hardships of the long marches across the deserts of Mesopotamia in the extreme heat of the summer.

'In fairness to the Turks it should be remembered that they were hard put to it to maintain their own field army in food and ammunition with their very inadequate shipping and land transport; and also that perhaps they scarcely understood that British and Indian soldiers cannot exist on the food on which a Turk will thrive, and that the British soldier in particular finds the heat of Mesopotamia excessively trying. Still, though our surrender was almost a matter of certainty for ten days or so before it occurred, the Turks do not appear to have made any arrangements for feeding and sheltering our men; and had it not been for the close proximity of the Relief Force and its ability to send up a large quantity of rations for the garrison of Kut after the surrender, the casualties from starvation and sickness would have increased to an appalling extent.'

After some days in Baghdad Captain Mousley and his companions were marched two miles to the railway station, loaded into a train and taken 80 miles to Samarra, where the line ended, and whence they continued on foot with one donkey to carry the kit of every two officers and one riding donkey for every three officers, so that those who were most ill or weakest did not have to cover the whole distance on foot. Mousley describes how they set out from Samarra on what has become a classic of human suffering, surpassed only by the horrors of the Burma Road:

'The sun was setting on the desert as our column of about forty British officers, a number of native (Indian) officers, and some sick men whom we took as orderlies, wound slowly over the scorching sand. Dust from the forward column blinded us . . . Lieutenant Lee-Bennett, with whom I shared a riding animal, collapsed after doing a mile or two, and so he rode most of the time. He had been very ill, whereas I was recovering, and, although racked with pain, I managed to keep going by holding onto a strap. At intervals in the hot night we halted. I shall never forget the impressiveness of the scene. Our long shadows reached far over the plain. For the most part we were silent men, and determination to get as far as possible was in everyone's heart, but it was an absolute gamble . . . Here and there an Indian Mussulman fell out for a few seconds, and with his head in the desert dust, paid his devotion to Allah. More than one of our guards did likewise. A glorious sky of red sailing clouds stretched above us . . .

'It was a feverish night, and as it wore on we found our strength giving out. To fall out was to be neglected and lost. One pressed on as in a sort of nightmare. Now and then a donkey fell or refused to budge and our orderlies had to be carried also. This meant casting kit. At last we reached the camping place, but there was no water. After an hour or two of broken sleep we were aroused by shouts of "Haidee" (Hurry!), "Yellah"(Get On) . . . our riding animal had vanished, so I had to walk. It was an awful march once the sun got up. In the distance a few sandstone hills appeared. Our tongues were swollen and our throats on fire as we at last staggered on to the river . . . After a rest of two hours we went on again over stony defiles.'

Another man who made the same march has described the conditions:

'The first column of our rank-and-file prisoners marched from Samarra on May 22nd and reached Mosul on June 3rd. It consisted of about 3000 men. No transport was provided except a few camels and donkeys for the sick, and the escort frequently used these animals, so that the sick men had to walk or die. The escort stole boots and clothing from the prisoners, and many of the latter had to march in strips of blankets wrapped round their feet. The usual ration given to our men was a double handful of atta (flour), a handful of wheat, a spoon of ghee and some salt. This was expected to last them for one, two or even three days. At Samarra another party of our men received a meat ration before starting for Mosul. The ration was one goat among 400 men. The prisoners were forced to sell the very clothes they stood in to avoid starvation. They were driven along by the escort like a herd of cattle. The meagre rations of atta and wheat were replaced in some cases by a few mouldy chuppatis. No firewood was ever issued to the prisoners for cooking their food.'

It must be remembered that officers were supposed to be paid the pay of their rank and so had to buy their own food and whatever they might need. Other ranks were due a certain ration. The provision of one and the other calls for a certain degree of efficient organization which was seldom achieved. As a result the officers were forced to sell their few belongings just to keep body and soul together and to feed the ORs whose rations were not always forthcoming.

When they reached Te Krit, they had covered a bare 100 miles of what was to become a journey of close on 1200 miles. Mousley continues his account:

'From here the trek became a daily affair. Men fell out and died or were left in some village. Donkeys collapsed and kit (valuable for selling or bartering, apart from its usefulness) had to be abandoned. From out of the darkness one heard moaning cries of "Marghaya, Sahib, Marghaya" (dying) from our Indian friends who could go no further. One looked into the night and saw the Arab fires, and knew the fate of him who fell out.

'. . . We made bivouac tents of our rugs by the river at which we fetched up each night. The country became a sandgrassy waste. Here and there were a few goats or sheep herded by the river. The rest was desert. At Kjan Keernina, a stopping place on the Tigris, we prepared for the long waterless march of which we had heard so much. We bought waterskins, cast spare kit, and with our few dates, chuppatis and

Overleaf: An Austrian staff car of World War I meeting a column of prisoners being marched back from the front.

the bones of our last meal for stew, for we could afford meat only once a week as our small pay from Baghdad was almost finished, we pressed on. It was a terrible march for sick men. Hour after hour we kept going, our thirst increasing and our water evaporating from the skins . . .

PREPARING TO
TAKE CAPTIVES

'The night of the first great waterless march we rested on the maidan, a hilly bare spot near some salt springs, and had a most entertaining time of it. Dust storms revolved around us and donkeys stamped over our heads as they stampeded . . . and shortly after, while it was still dark, we were hurried on . . . The waterless march continued through dust and heat. Donkey after donkey collapsed. Our last drop of water was evaporating, so we drank it. At last after some hours we looked down over a depression and the cry "mai, mai" (water) came from the guards ahead. The Tigris lay far below.

'An hour or so afterwards we reached Shergat, that in old times was Asshur — the Assyrian capital of the 13th century BC . . . I was feeling very weakened and could not sleep for pain in my spine, but hoped to get through as the waterless march was over.

'Malaria returned the second night, and with a temperature of 105° I heard we were off. I felt appallingly unsteady and my head throbbed with every movement of the donkey, as it does in such cases. I was lucky to have any donkey at all . . .

'We went on through the nights and through the days; through dust-storms and heat, by night passing the fires of Arabs who awaited the stragglers, sometimes camping by Bedouin tents or pebbly watercourses, always following the trail of dead, for every mile or so one saw mounds of our dead soldiers by the wayside. We left Hammamali, a village of sulphur baths, on the 14th June, and stumbling over rocky ground for some hours we reached far-famed Mosul, and with great delight saw again a few trees. Then appeared the mounds of Nineveh and those of the palace of the great King Sardanapalus . . . In the foreground we saw a great tomb which we were told was John the Baptist's, and Alexander's great battlefield of Arbela lay on the eastern plain. On the 10th a few tiny donkeys were given us for riding animals, about enough to allow one officer out of six a ride one hour in three . . . For transport we were shown a set of a dozen untrained, wild and unharnessed camels, altogether the most savage and nasty brutes I have ever seen. They were unapproachable and snapped and gyrated and then trotted away . . .

'I was almost two stones underweight, and very unwell from the long bout of colitis, my digestion quite out of gear, weak from want of nourishment and my shell-bruise, not to mention continual pain from my eyes. Yet with all the exertion and sleepless nights, so fascinating was movement after a long inaction that I managed to get along.

'Each day before dawn we were up, and after a breakfast of tea, black bread, a small piece of cheese and two figs, or generally only raisins, we prepared to leave . . . On this trek we lost the sense of time. Sometimes we marched by day, but generally in the evening, and well on into the night. But for us time was not . . . I knew two seasons only: when we walked and when we did not . . . We have had to rely on provisions we brought with us and live chiefly on raisins. At Demir Kapu we finished the most strenuous march I have ever done. It was a dry, waterless stretch of forty kms over parched ground with not even salt water springs en route . . . At our next halting-place a dust-storm descended on our camp in the night. I have been in dust storms in various places, but this was of a new order. With a roar like thunder a deluge of sand fell upon us, travelling terrifically fast. It tore down bivouacs, carried off tents and valises, pulled up picketing pegs, and rolled even heavy pots hundreds of yards off, where they were buried in the sand and many lost. We could not stand against it any more than against an incoming tide. One buried one's head and lay with all one's weight on one's kit . . . My chief loss was my topee . . . The next day my improvised head-gear of a towel proved inadequate, and I went down with an awful attack of sunstroke . . . I arrived at Nisibin feeling very ill and feverish . . . I set out yesterday for the hospital to recover a topee, as I heard a British officer had died there . . . through an opening in the wall I saw a sight that staggered the imagination.

'A bare strip of ground ran down to the river some two hundred yards off. Along the wall, protected only by a few scanty leaves and loose grass flung over some tatti work of branches through which the fierce sun streamed with unabated violence, I saw some human forms which no one but one acquainted with the phenomenon of the trek could possibly recognize as British soldiery. They were wasted to wreathes of skin hanging upon a bone frame. For the most part they were stark naked except for a rag round their loins, their garments having been sold to buy food, bread, milk and medicine. Their eyes were white with the death hue. Their sunken cheeks were covered with the unshaven growth of weeks. One had just died and two or three corpses just been removed, the Turkish attendant no doubt having heard of the approach of an officers' column. But the corpses had lain there for days. Some of the men were too weak to move. The result of the collection of filth and the unsanitary state in the centre of which these men lay in a climate like this can be imagined. Water was not regularly supplied to them, and those unable to walk had to crawl to the river for water. One could see their tracks through the grime and dirt . . . Other forms near by I thought dead, but they moved unconsciously again. One saw the beehive phenomenon of flies which swarmed by the million going in and out of living men's open mouths.

'*Rase-el-Ain, July 4th*. I am thankful to Providence that I am lucky enough to write this heading. At last we arrived in the wretched village, but as I write I hear a locomotive puffing and puffing. We are on the railhead. No sailor after being tossed amid shipwreck in a frantic ocean ever felt happier to be in port than we do, to realize the long march is done. There are other marches ahead over mountains, but they are short we hear. The desert is crossed. We left Nisibin on June 29th at 6.30 pm. The pace of the column was coming down to about two miles, often less, an hour. The local Arabs seemed wilder, and we had to keep together as one party of Turks had been recently massacred outright . . . For the stragglers it was certain death at the Arab's hands.

'Suddenly some time after sunset, we were just preparing to settle down by the station for the night when a train drew up. With some other subalterns I found a small place for a bed in a truck. There was a space of four feet by two for each of us. We stuffed our legs anywhere and slept. The train started and we awoke. The doors of the truck were open. We watched the desert go by, thankful beyond expression, mysti-fied at this extraordinary change, the conveyance of dying men without

If you were slightly wounded or ill, fortune might provide a seat in a farmer's wagon to take you into captivity. This photograph taken in Galicia in World War I shows some of the lucky ones. The only sour face is that of the peasant who is having to drive them instead of attending to his farm.

their own effort. The terrible bumps and the state of the trucks were nothing. It was a train.'

The railway removed much of the misery of their long trek into captivity, except that the tunnels through the mountains were not yet complete and the prisoners had to cross the Taurus by road. Thanks to a German air force officer, who was engaged to a girl in England, and the vigorous reprimand he gave the Turkish commandant, carts were provided to take the prisoners' baggage and to allow them an occasional ride on this trek. Once over the mountains, they returned to the railway and were taken to Angora and northwards to the camp at Kastamuni.

When all these different accounts of POWs' journeys to their places of confinement are compared, it is obvious that however hard or however little the authorities concerned have tried to comply with the international conventions in force or even just the dictates of humanity, local conditions and the local availability of materials, transport and supplies have ultimately determined the prisoners' treatment.

It is not always easy to be humane, even for those who try. One might expect that an aggressor, who has been preparing his attack and is confident of victory, would have prepared measures in advance for looking after the prisoners he expected to take. There is, for example, evidence that the Germans expected to take two to three million Soviet prisoners in 1941, since the planned blitz pincer movements would, if successful, entrap whole armies. (The actual total was close on three and a half million). Because of this, the POW Section had been instructed to recruit staffs for 25 reception and regular camps each capable of accommodating upwards of 40 000 prisoners. But there is no evidence of similar action — beyond the divisional quartermaster's normal provision of a POW cage and basic equipment — having been taken to deal with French and British POWs, for the simple reason that it had been assumed that, when it came to it, there would be no war with either France or England. The prisoners actually captured in a sense took the authorities by surprise. This is borne out by the experience of Captain John Mansell in May 1940. His diary reads thus:

'21st. Hid up with my party in wood adjoining Doullens-Abbeville road. Made recce on road teeming with traffic. French boy fetching washing from a line by a cottage sees some of us, runs back so frightening kids, and in a few minutes we are surrounded. No food since 5.30 yesterday afternoon. We were marched off with troops to a nearby vehicle park of German transport — approx. 8.30–9.0 a.m. After about an hour marched off along Doullens road to St Riquier. Here put in a church. Produced my Emergency Ration and doled it round. Later separated from troops and joined a party of officers — including Francis Chancellor and Bill Renton. Troops I think went ahead and we followed them, marching about ten miles along the same road. I watched a German officer inspecting a dump of British rifles and doing all he could to break one across his knee in disdain. Some scraps of pork are found for the troops. We are shoved into a sort of attic. After a time we are told to get into some lorries in which we are to be taken a short way to the village where we are to have some food and sleep. Some of us get on board.

'It was by this time night and far from a meal or a nearby village; we don't stop until we get to St Quentin. I slept most of the way and only remember the silhouette of the German guard in back of lorry — there were 20 of us in it — and leaving my Dunhill pipe in it. Still wearing steel helmet and having gas cape, haversack and respirator case — binocular and compass cases, water bottle and webbing belt. Had buried other items in wood by Vauchelle before leaving.

'22nd. Arrived St Quentin 3.30 a.m. in our lorries. No food. Slept on first floor of a garage and slept like a log. Joined here overnight by Majors Wilby, Clout, etc. When we woke up had a sort of semi wash in a horrible little w.c. In an appalling scramble manage to collect two biscuits and a few cough drops and some cold coffee. Pack up and are pushed off into the Square — flooded with privates, mostly French. Eventually an English band of about 30 officers takes up the rear of this vast snake which starts to wind its way out of the town. All the shops have been looted and place in an incredible shambles.

'Marched 20 odd miles to Guise. No food on the way. Endless stream of German troops moving in opposite direction — looking very efficient, smart and fit. Always met by astonished looks as we were presumably first British to be seen. "Chamberline" — "Churchill" — "Tommies" — "For you the war is ended" — etc, etc. Six foot-four of Bill Renton just in front supremely disdainful. Occasional halts for water but too tired to bother to fight for it. Always promise of food at next halt. Can never see the head of the column. Planes dive on us and scream down the line over our heads, with occasional burst of machine-gun just as a cheerio biff. Definitely fatal to fall out in rear. Some

Overleaf: The Japanese captors bow low as former American POWs file past to freedom. Conditions in Japanese camps varied considerably.

marching shoeless and sockless. Guise a shamble of ruined and burning buildings and burned-out tanks.

'Finally enter a field in late evening. Find some rhododendron bushes and have sufficient desire for privacy to hide amongst them and coopy down. Here Bill Renton and I and Chang Ebbutt find a spot and snuggle up together on the ground and go to sleep. Woken about midnight for a drop of soup. See horse brought in and killed and roasted — but we didn't get any.

'25th. No breakfast. Travelled by truck via Phillipeville, Givet, Rochefort to Marche (still Belgium). Here we were first of all put inside a sort of courtyard and had some good food — barley soup and coffee. Maybe it was a school yard. This was, I think, about midday. Again we thought we were leaving after the meal, but we were taken into a church, where we eventually spent the night. This was ghastly. Met Barrie Grayson here. Shaving on the altars; washing everywhere; men relieving themselves everywhere, church or no church. Confessional not comfortable for sleeping in. Pitiful sight of the French Padré arriving at his church . . .

'26th. Only food $1\frac{1}{2}$ biscuits between 8 men. By truck through Ardennes . . . Flung into a room feet deep in straw. Courtyard alive with thousands of French and Belgian POW. About 3 latrines in constant use. Not a hope . . . Left in evening and entrained about 9.0 p.m. Put first into a cattle truck, 65 of us . . . We are moved into a compartment. Hellish crowded. Cattle truck might have been more comfortable. But there was a lavatory. We get some bread and paste. Sleep that night in turn on the floor and in the little luggage racks.

'28th. Arrived at Neuburgsdorf at 6.0 a.m. Detrained. Marched to enormous Camp some miles away. Stalag IV B. All notices in Polish . . .'

MARCHING ON AN EMPTY STOMACH

Compare this relatively 'uncomfortable' journey with that undertaken by Lieutenant Solczynski who was wounded and captured by the Russians during the Polish campaign of September 1939 and then imprisoned at Artemovsk in the Ukraine until the Russians evacuated it in September 1941, abandoning all their stores but taking all their prisoners.

'One fine day we were paraded, to the number of a thousand, drawn up in fours, given a kilo of bread and salt fish per man, and then ordered to march.

'Such was the manner in which we left our prison, guarded by men of the 207th Convoy Regiment, mounted and on foot, and accompanied by police dogs. We had also with us eighty women, among them a fair-haired Polish girl with a worn face, who was, I think, a prostitute from Lvov.

'. . . We marched without a rest until six that evening, along a bad road, which was thick in deep, clinging mud. At last they halted us. We were divided into close-packed groups and told to sit down. We were given nothing to eat or drink. One of the Russian prisoners asked for some water. "Here's water for you!" said one of the mounted soldiers, and began striking at him with his sabre. Neither that day nor the next were we given so much as a drop of water to quench our thirst. A senior officer of the convoy made it quite clear to us from the outset that if he finished the journey with 5 per cent of his prisoners, it would be more than adequate. I suffered terribly from thirst. I put a piece of bread in my mouth and started to munch it, but a quarter of an hour passed before I could swallow it, so dry was my throat. My saliva had become white and viscous.

'From the very first day of our march, the guards made use of their dogs. They did not unleash them at once because the beasts would have leaped at the men and torn them to pieces. But they led them up to any men who were lagging, or who had stopped, not wanting or not being able to go any further. The dogs tore at their clothing and bit their flesh, so that the prisoners struggled to their feet in a desperate effort to keep going. After marching without a rest from 10 am to 6 pm, we were again halted. We remained without shelter, and crowded together without food or drink, until six o'clock the next morning. It was bitterly cold, and about 3 am it started to rain. At last the column resumed its march.

'We were still given no water. Hunger — because what bread I had left stuck in my throat — and terrible thirst so exhausted me that I had to go slowly. A heavy weight of mud clung to my feet. Black spots began to dance in front of my eyes, and as soon as we started to go uphill, I collapsed.

'I remained where I had fallen, stretched in the mud. When at last I struggled to my feet, one of the Polish officers came up to me, and slipped into my hand a few pieces of sugar which he was keeping in reserve. They saved my life. The black spots stopped dancing, and leaning on the arm of the man next to me, I was able to resume the march.

'The Russian prisoners who were with us could be divided into two categories. The greater part of them were bandits. They kept together in gangs and terrorised the other prisoners.

'Our march was only two days old when they began to attack several of my companions, stripping them of everything they had. They made off with my last piece of bread.

'About ten o'clock the snow began to fall, and it was sheer heaven for us to quench our thirst with great handfuls of the stuff. That day we covered 30 kilometres. Seventy of us were crowded into a room measuring 18 feet by 21. About a hundred of us were in a slightly larger room nearby. As usual we were given nothing to eat or drink. The latrines would accommodate ten persons only; the rest had to manage as best we could, with the result that those close to the door were ankle-deep in excrement.'

A 'COMPLETELY DISGRACEFUL' PROCEDURE

Lieutenant Solczynski finally reached his POW camp on November 22. His was one of two columns together amounting to some 2000 men, of whom only 550 survived and of these ten or 15 were dying every day in the quarters prepared for them.

At about the same time as Lieutenant Solczyski made his march, Russell Braddon coming from a different hemisphere — Australia — was fighting in jungle rather than steppe, but he was dealing with men whose attitude to war was strikingly similar. He has described his surrender and subsequent journey into captivity:

'I didn't wait to see what happened. I was off at once, sprinting wildly, towards the jungle on the left. Beside me, I was aware without seeing him, ran Hugh. Cursing myself for every fool in the world, I thought yearningly of those four beautiful hand grenades now lying uselessly beside a canal on the other side of Yong Peng.

' "Stop there," I heard the officer's clear voice directed at us, "stop and surrender or we'll all be shot" — and my absurd army training made me falter for a second and look back. I saw Herc already bleeding from a wound in the arm; and Sandshoes and the sergeant lying on the ground; and the officer standing quite still, the sigs looking at him questioningly and Harry in outrage. Just for a second we faltered. As in any race, when one falters, it was then too late. The path to the jungle was cut by a Jap soldier with a tommy gun. We stood still, our only chance lost. Then, very slowly, very foolishly and with a sense of utter unreality, I put up my hands.

'At that moment all that occurred to me was that this procedure was completely disgraceful. I have not — since then — changed my mind. I have no doubt at all that I should have continued running. One does not win battles by standing still and extending the arms upwards in the hope that one's foes have read the Hague Convention concerning the treatment of Prisoners of War. It was unfortunate that the army had trained sufficiently neither to disobey instantly and without hesitation, nor to obey implicitly and without compunction. Accordingly, I had done neither: and now I stood in the recognized pose of one who optimistically seeks mercy from a conqueror whose reputation is for being wholly merciless.

'The enemy patrol closed in on us. Black-whiskered men, with smutty eyes and the squat pudding faces of bullies. They snatched off our watches first of all — and then belted us with rifle butts because these did not point to the north as they swung them around under the ludicrous impression that they were compasses . . . Then they tied us up with wire, lashing it round our wrists, which were crossed behind our backs and looped to our throats. They prodded us to the edge of a drain in the rubber. We sat with our legs in it, while they set their machine guns up facing us and about ten yards away . . .

' "We must die bravely," said the officer desperately — at which the sergeant howled for mercy. Howled and pleaded, incredibly craven . . . We sat, the nine of us, side by side, on the edge of our ready-dug grave.

'The Japanese machine gunner lay down and peered along his barrel. It was my twenty-first birthday and I was not happy.'

Fortunately, when the machine-gun fired it was at a fleeing figure on the hillside, who was quickly caught, dragged downhill to the others and tied up with his own puttees. There were about 15 Japanese who after conferring together apparently thought better of killing their prisoners, whom they finally prodded to their feet with bayonets and they then set out on what was to be 'a long and rather unpleasant march'. They were used as pathfinders through a minefield and marched briskly all day, a day of harsh heat during which they were allowed neither water nor rests.

'At about four in the afternoon our captors sat down under a banana tree to eat. We were kept standing in the sun on a hard-baked track which ran through the small clearing. We were not guarded with much attention. On the other hand, we were too securely shackled, hand and foot, for all of us to unloose ourselves and escape. Since we had agreed that only a joint escape attempt would be made . . .'

In a fury Russell Braddon tore his wrists and hands free and demanded water, which eventually a Malay brought and Braddon distributed, a couple of mouthfuls a time to each, the sergeant (who had earlier drunk all the milk in a coconut himself) being served last. Finally, the Japanese officer realized that Braddon was now untied and spoke to one of his men:

'That individual rose to his feet, did up his fly-buttons, put on both his belts, mopped his skull and placed on it first his cap, then his helmet, and then walked slowly towards me. Quite dispassionately he tied my hands behind my back again, looped the rope around my throat and down to the wrists once more. Then he ordered the sergeant over and joined the loose ends of my rope to the knot which secured his wrists. Then he dragged the two of us to Hugh and tied Hugh to the other side of the sergeant. The other seven men were tied up in a three and a four. Then he returned slowly to the banana tree, took off his helmet and his cap, removed his two belts, undid his fly, sat down again in the shade. For twenty minutes they murmured quietly among themselves . . . Then they rose — we were on the march again.

'We marched the rest of that day and much of the night in grim silence. Marched with a speed and sureness that was astounding. We did not once see a road; we were usually in jungle; when we did hit a clearing, it came as no surprise to the Japs, who were instantly greeted by a Malay who had hot food ready. This clockwork organization of fifth column sympathizers and the time-table marching was almost incredible when one realized that the Japs who guarded us had been in Malaya only six weeks and that they had spent the preceding seven years fighting in China . . . At midnight we halted and the patrol slept — leaving us always heavily guarded. It was unnecessary. We slept, too. Nothing could have kept us awake — not even being trussed together, all nine of us, into an immovable and inflexible lump of humanity. At dawn we were off again. The Japs had washed, eaten and drunk — but we received nothing.

'At midday we passed a large formation of bicycle troops. They carried small mortars, civilian clothes, mortar ammunition and rifles. We were severely mishandled and each of us was punched and kicked a hundred times. In addition, some of us had our boots taken from us and marched, thenceforward, barefooted. The jungle is not kind to those who walk in bare feet.'

They came across a further lot of bicycle troops and received the same treatment, before marching on. They came to where a British convoy had been ambushed by the Japs. Only 30 of the British survived to be added to the Australian contingent. Here they stayed for 48 hours during which time they received one distribution of water, which gave them about three mouthfuls each — plus four coconuts. Through a hole in the wall of his 'chicken-coop' Braddon managed to scrape a double handful of fly-blown rice off the Japanese garbage heap and this gave them about a spoonful each. At the end of 48 hours they were herded into a truck (British) and driven off, reaching Ayer Hitam, where the superficially wounded were given some inadequate treatment by the Japanese and the seriously wounded were presumably killed off for no one ever saw them again.

'We slept the night in a school which reeked of death. In the morning one of the British soldiers produced a safety razor and a blade. About thirty of us shaved with it. There was a well in the school which provided water for shaving and bathing and (in spite of rumours of a corpse in it) drinking. We were questioned, beaten up and moved to

Batu Pahat. At Batu Pahat we were questioned, beaten up and moved to Gemas. At Gemas we were questioned, beaten up (with special fury because there the Australian 2/30th Battalion had staged a particularly successful ambush) and put into a cattle truck on a train . . . We had now been ten days with virtually no food at all and eight of us had marched about 180 miles in that time . . . The train stopped thirty-six hours later at a bomb-wrecked station which the Malay Volunteers told us was Kuala Lumpur. We were marched from the station through the city; and the march was made unforgettable by the stoning and spitting meted out by a native population which had only a fortnight before been hysterically pro-British . . .

'A mile from the station high dun-coloured walls looked down at us. We turned a corner and marched beside them. Huge doors opened and we passed through them. The doors closed. We were prodded into a small courtyard and that, too, was closed. Inside the courtyard we found 700 men. It had been designed to provide exercise for 30 female convicts. In it, and the cells for those 30 female convicts, we 700 were now to live, sleep, cook, excrete, wash and die.'

During the fighting in Korea much later, an American medical captain accompanied his unit captured by the Chinese on its march to Death Valley, a camp 65 miles south of Pyoktong on the river Yalua. This march that took 25 days Bilderman has described in his *March to Calumny*:

'Within two or three days after capture there were about 100 prisoners in Captain X's group, of which ten to twenty were slightly wounded. No medical treatment was available. The prisoners had been stripped of all medical supplies and equipment and many of them had had their overcoats and shoes taken away. This group was joined by other groups during the march and by the time they arrived at Death Valley, there were approximately 500 prisoners in the group. The officers and enlisted men were separated on the third or fourth day of the march. The marching was done at night. This had an adverse effect on the men. The long marching period made them perspire and they became very cold during the long break. During the day they stayed in Korean mud huts. Twenty-five men were crowded into an 8 foot by 10 foot room, too crowded for them to lie down. They ate in the morning about an hour after stopping and again in the evening about an hour before departure. Food consisted of about four ounces of cracked corn. No utensils were available. Water came from wells, rice paddies and melted snow. Two-thirds of the group developed bloody dysentry during the march. The men became weak and the weaker were helped by the stronger as long as possible; then the weaker ones would be left with a guard.

'Frequently shots were heard and then the guard, who had been left with the prisoners, would return to the column. Approximately fifty persons were lost on the march.'

ORDEAL AFTER PEARL HARBOR

But the most gruesome experience of conditions 'in transit' is that of the American POWs recorded in Sidney Stewart's *Give Us This Day*. These Americans had been captured by the Japanese after Pearl Harbor and kept in the Philippines until the war began to go wrong for the Japanese, and the avenging American forces had actually landed in the islands. It was then decided to evacuate the American POWs to Japan. Sidney Stewart and his companions were marched down to the port and put abroad a Japanese liner. All the accommodation for passengers was occupied by Japanese civilians and the wives and children of officers and officials so that the POWs were herded into the holds. That in which Sydney Stewart found himself was large enough to accommodate perhaps one hundred, but into it 600 were crowded. They were packed so tightly that if a man fainted, he could not fall. They were all weak and undernourished. Now they were told that it would take the liner ten days to get to Japan — ten days in such conditions! It became hotter and hotter in the hold. Men began begging for water. There was none available and the guard told them to shut up or the hatch would be put over the hold and then they would get no air. Men were now being maddened and their screams were those of the crazed. Some were laughing hysterically, high-pitched laughter broken by sobs. Here and there could be heard mumbled prayers. Then they began fighting and suddenly there was more room, for the dead and fainting slid down under the feet of those still erect.

One of Sydney Stewart's companions had been so weak they had scarcely been able to drag him down to the port and aboard the Japanese liner. In the hold they had him wedged upright between them, and thus he died. He was free, though they had lost their long struggle to keep him with them. One of them wept. They debated what to do with the body. They could not bear the thought of letting him be trampled beneath the feet there, yet they had not the strength to hold him up for any length of time, let alone ten days. 'Finally, we laid him beneath us and Rass stood on him.'

All around them were strange choking noises mingling with the screams and sounds of fighting. Men were cutting each other's throats and drinking the blood.

> 'A few feet away I saw two men grappling. In the gloom I recognized who they were. They were father and son. I remembered how they had protected and cared for each other in the years past. They were both West Point graduates. The son was killing his father. I could see the look in the father's eyes. A look of compassion and pity for the son who was a maniac. Then the father screamed. His screams rent the hold . . . I knew that he was dead. The son — God, he was drinking his father's blood.'

Incredibly, there were survivors, due solely to the fact that the voyage to Japan was never completed, for the ship came under attack from the air and had to be run aground in the shallows. Those with the strength to swim took to the water and, though machine-gunned from the shore, some reached land and lived to tell the ghastly tale.

It is obvious that in all these cases, if the captors had really wished to treat their captives humanely, to say nothing of protecting their lives, very much more could have been done for them, but when there are not enough resources for the march (food, transport, medicine) to go round, whose lives do you save? What is a war crime in one set of eyes, may be a necessary, though regrettable act in another's. In wars between different races, captors have on occasion regarded their captives not as fellow human beings but almost as sub-human, however unjustified this attitude may be. Perhaps the Romans encountering those strange painted people, the Picts, for the first time, or those who first saw the naked Indians of Tierra del Fuego, felt that way about them: that they were expendable, creatures to whom the laws of Rome, the rules of chivalry or of Christian behaviour just did not apply. In such cases, the POW, the most unwanted person on earth, is in for a sorry time indeed.

C H A P T E R   5

LIVING CONDITIONS

The POW should, according to the current conventions, be properly housed in a district which is not unhealthy, and the dormitory accommodation and food must be the same as for depot troops of the detaining power. The camp must be hygienic and must have facilities for washing and the benefit of being out-of-doors. So much for the theory. The last two world wars have shown that in practice there is more likelihood of a soldier losing his life in a POW camp, or on the way there, than on the battlefield.

One of the earliest descriptions of the conditions under which POWs were forced to live is in Thucydides' history of the Peloponnesian Wars. He tells how the Athenian prisoners captured at Syracuse (BC 413) were put in the stone (marble) quarries there and:

> 'were crowded within a small compass in a hollow place, and being unsheltered, they were at first distressed by the suffocating closeness and heat of the sun, and afterwards by the cold of the autumnal nights. From their want of space they were obliged to do everything in the same place, whilst the corpses of those who died from sickness or wounds were piled up together, and emitted an intolerable stench. They were also tormented with hunger and thirst, for during eight months they received daily only one cotyle (about half a pint) of water and two of corn; and, in short, there was no misery which men could experience in such a place that did not fall to their lot. For 70 days they were thus immured together, and then they were all sold except the Athenians, Siceliots and Italiots. The total number of prisoners was 7000.'

The Athenians and the others not sold were kept in the quarries for a further six months, receiving presumably the same ration of food and liquid which was half that commonly allowed to a slave. Those that survived were then sold off in their turn.

De Joinville has described how the Crusaders captured by the Saracens were held captive in the holds of their galleys in conditions little different from those in the holds of the *Altmark* and *Kormoran* in World War II. We know in what dreadful conditions many of those awaiting payment of ransoms were kept during the Middle Ages. Others, of course, those of high birth who had had the good fortune to be captured by their peers, were treated as welcome paying guests — and pay they did! — and so suffered nothing but the discomfort of having their freedom of movement restricted and in being separated from their families and friends.

As warfare became more professional this respect for one's prisoner became more general. The English sea captain, Richard Hawkins, after negotiating the Straits of Magellan in the spring of 1594, capturing five Spanish ships in Valparaiso and being chased northwards up the coast, was finally caught by the Spaniards in Atacames Bay in modern Ecuador. There followed three days of ferocious fighting at the end of which Hawkins found that he had 8 ft of water in the hold, many of his men killed and more wounded, while the rest, who had had recourse to spirits as a substitute for rest and refreshment, were 'mad drunk', and so he surrendered to the Spanish commander, Don Beltran de Castro. Don Beltran took them all to Panama, where the wounded prisoners were 'healed', so presumably those who survived the journey to Panama recovered.

Hawkins' captor offered to send to England whatever letters Hawkins cared to write. Some of those he wrote were to arrange for payment of his ransom. The one he wrote to his wife told her that he was the prisoner of a 'most honourable prince who treats me more like a brother than a prisoner.' He went on to say that de Castro and his wife 'are much delighted in hawking and hunting the wild boar and other beasts. I assure myself that if it lay only in the hands of Don Beltran de Castro my ransom should be nothing else but horses, hawks and hounds of Ireland.' It was Hawkins' misfortune that these first letters were never delivered and as a result he had to wait a long time for his ransom to arrive, though it did so in the end.

The ransom seems to have gone out of fashion in the latter half of the eighteenth century, by which time the system of exchange had again been fully developed and most people preferred to await their turn for exchange rather than to ruin their families by buying their freedom perhaps only a few months earlier. Under this system officers, who gave their *parole d'honneur* not to try to escape or engage in any activities detrimental to their captors, were allowed to live outside the prison camp provided that they did not travel further than a certain distance from where they lived, that they returned to their quarters by certain hours and reported to a local authority every so often. Otherwise they could live as their means allowed. Each received a certain subsistence allowance normally determined and paid by his own government; this was usually somewhat meagre and had to be supplemented either by making things to sell to the local civilians or with money sent from home, if the person concerned had the means. (There seems never to have been any difficulty in transferring the money even from an enemy country.)

In Sweden in the early eighteenth century Russian officers were given quarters and clothing, but received no subsistence allowance, as the Russian government would not agree to refund it. Many of them had private means and rented furnished flats for themselves. Some could even afford to keep a carriage. In Russia at the same time, where ordinary soldiers were fed and housed by the Tsar and in return expected to work for the Tsar, the officers

POW — Prisoner of War
— PG — Prisionero
Guerra — are daubed on
the walls of this shed in
the Falklands to indicate
its change of use from
sheep shearing to
housing prisoners. It
served as temporary
accommodation for
Argentine POWs, the
conscript soldiers who
are seen inside the shed,
amusing themselves in
different ways. A good
deal of sheep-shearing
debris still litters the
floor.

The guard tower of a POW camp in Russia during World War I.

were quartered in wooden houses, often put up in haste as the need arose to accommodate a sudden influx of POWs. A contemporary engraving of Tobolsk shows at least 200 such box-like houses built on the low ground between the city proper and the river in which Swedish POWs were housed. If one of these officers wished to go into the town to buy something, the Swedish duty captain had to seek the permission of the Russian commander of the camp who provided a strong guard under an officer to accompany the shopper. Prisoners were allowed to visit each other in their different barracks, and they were allowed to go to a Swedish church every Sunday. Here again they had to be accompanied by a Russian officer (at least a lieutenant) and an interpreter (in case the sermon was not confined to religion, but turned to plans for escape) and a strong guard armed with muskets. After the service they could go to an eating-house and dine at their own expense, then go to evening service and afterwards straight back 'to prison'.

For the ordinary soldier it was different. Conditions in which they were housed and worked were such that in the long run (and for many captivity was indeed lengthy) they died in considerable numbers, both in Sweden and Russia. Some Russian commanders even sold Swedes captured in small parties as serfs and these were never heard of again.

The picture of the paroled officer a hundred years later was little different: French prisoners on parole in Leek (Staffordshire) during the Napoleonic Wars are said to 'have received all courtesy and hospitality from the principal inhabitants of the town and neighbourhood. Those with good private means used to dine out in full uniform, each with his body servant stationed behind his chair.'

There were other prisoners on parole in Melrose, Roxburghshire, and Sir Walter Scott used to have some of them to dine in his house, Abbotsford, two miles outside the town, to do which he had to move the milestone to just beyond the entrance to his house, as otherwise they would have been out of bounds. Other prisoners in Cornwall are recorded as having been seen at shoots, at Bodmin races, dining at houses well outside the limits set by their parole.

The conditions of life for the other prisoners were very different, but it must be remembered that the burden of feeding, clothing and housing such a huge number put an enormous strain on the ingenuity and resources of their 'hosts'.

CAMP IN BRITAIN

By 1799 there were just under 26 000 French POWs in Britain, which number more than filled all the available accommodation in the country's fortresses and prisons, so special ships (hulks) were called into service and stationed at Portsmouth, Plymouth and the Medway. Even this was insufficient and the government had to start building. The first POW prison camp as such was at Norman Cross near Shelton. Another was built at Perth in Scotland and a third later on Dartmoor, by which time the number of POWs had risen to 50 000. Between 1803 and 1814, the second stage of the Napoleonic Wars, there were no less than 123 000 POWs of various nationalities, while in 1793 and 1814 the number had been close to 200 000.

Quarters of some of the Russian POWs confined at Lewes during the Crimean War. These were so well treated that, when they were finally sent home, they officially thanked the people of Lewes for their hospitality.

When the need for extra accommodation became obvious in 1796, a time when the British felt confident of defeating the Dutch fleet, which had recently put to sea, and the capture of a large number of Dutch prisoners seemed imminent, the authorities acted with commendable vigour and disregard for red tape, and set about building the prisons at Norman Cross and Perth. The prison at Norman Cross was designed to house 5000 POWs. Apart from administrative buildings, a hospital, guard rooms, etc, there

Two Germans, not in Siberia, but in Central Europe. Cold can be cleansing in that it dries up mud and is a great aid to hygiene, though — increasing the need for fuel and clothing — it provides its own problems.

were 16 two-storeyed wooden barracks, each 100 ft long and 22 ft wide, roofed with red tiles. The frames were made in London and sent down to Norman Cross, where an army of carpenters erected them and put up weather boarding, working seven days a week (those who refused to work on Sunday were dismissed) all within the space of four months, during which time wells were dug, quadrangles paved and latrines built. The system was one of elevated seats with a soil cart standing below, this being removed as required and replaced with another. There was no sewage or drainage system as we know it, if only because no one knew how long the camp would be occupied and the extra work would probably have delayed completion.

Each barrack was divided into three 'chambers' on each floor; the ceiling of the ground floor was 12 ft high and this allowed three tiers of hammocks to be hung. It must have been quite an acrobatic feat getting into the topmost layer, but as many of the early prisoners were sailors from the Dutch and French fleets, perhaps they were accustomed to it. The first floor ceiling was only 8 ft high and so could accommodate only two layers of hammocks. Each prisoner was allowed a palliasse (or straw mattress), a rug and a bolster. Each day one in 12 men were on fatigue duty, which included preparing their own food from the rations supplied, probably using local peat as a fuel, and this was done in messes usually of 12.

By the time it was decided to build Dartmoor to help relieve the congestion, the price of timber had soared because none was coming in from the Baltic ports. Corrugated iron had not yet been invented, bricks were not made anywhere near enough to the moor to be a practical proposition, and so the prison was built of the granite which lay everywhere about the moor and could be had for the cost of carting and dressing it. This work was done largely by Cornish masons, who, halfway through, demanded more money and got it. The accommodation was primitive enough, but tolerable when the weather was decent, which it was not always. The winter of 1813–14 was perhaps the worst for 50 years.

On New Year's night:

'the buckets in the prison froze solid in four hours. The running stream that supplied all the buildings with water was ice to the bottom; the prisoners quenched their thirst with snow, and huddled together at night to prevent being frozen; their breath, condensing on the granite, covered the walls with a film of ice. Then it began to snow, and on January 19th the snow was four feet deep on the level, and the drifts reached to the tops of the walls. No sentry could face the weather on the military walk, and the guards were all withdrawn to the guard-house. The position of the prison had become most serious. More than 9000 prisoners and 1500 soldiers and civilians were entirely dependent for their food on the waggon road to Plymouth,' and this was blocked. Emergency rations were issued, but of these only ten days supply remained, nor could they be drawn upon until Captain Shortland at the head of 200 French prisoners and all the guards and civilians that could be spared had spent a whole day cutting a road to the storehouse. At midnight on January 19th, when the weather was at its worst, eight Americans, seeing the sentries withdrawn, improvised a ladder and scaled the boundary wall. Ill-luck had led them to choose a spot close to the guard-house, and becoming entangled in the wire of the alarm bells, they alerted the guard, who turned out in time to capture seven of them. For these perhaps it was a happy accident, for men wandering half-clad over the moor on such a night could hardly have survived. The eighth ploughed his way doggedly through the snow till he came to a lonely

These Russian prisoners have dug themselves holes in which to shelter from the elements while awaiting transport, another instance of sheer weight of numbers breaking the fragile machinery for dealing with POWs. It must be remembered that the easiest and most convenient way of dealing with them would have been to have done nothing and left them to fend for themselves and perish. Alexander the Great would have approved such behaviour, but in the twentieth century it is unthinkable.

hut. The moormen, knowing that none but escaped prisoners could be out in such weather, secured him and brought him back, and the eight men were put in solitary confinement, where they remained for ten days on two-thirds allowance. They were no more wretched than the rest, who passed this awful fortnight bare-legged, with salt-beef and snow for food and drink, without fire or sufficient clothing, overrun with vermin and decimated by sickness.'

HULKS AND THE AMERICAN CIVIL WAR

Fifty years later, during the American Civil War, conditions were certainly little or no better, although neither side needed to use hulks or build special camps, but were able to use empty tobacco warehouses (Libby Prison) or vacant apartments (Capitol Prison, Washington):

'All prison camps were death traps in that war. They were over-crowded, reeking from lack of sanitation, badly policed; housing was bad, food was worse, and medical care was sometimes worst of all. This was due less to any active ill-will on either side than to the general, unin-tended brutality and heartlessness of war. Army life in those days was rough, even under the best conditions, and disease killed many more men than bullets killed; in a prison camp this roughness was inevitably intensified (26,486 Southerners and 22,576 Northerners died in prison camps) even though nobody really meant it so.'

Such is the difficulty, perhaps the impossibility, of treating prisoners of war decently and humanely as soon as their numbers get up into the tens of thou-sands. When they are being counted in hundreds of thousands, as was the case in World War I and to a much greater extent in World War II, the logis-tical difficulties alone of housing them seem to have been insuperable, however much good will there may, or may not, have been. Never before have such large numbers of men been taken prisoner in individual battles as on the Eastern (German/Soviet) Front in World War II, and, although the planned *blitzkrieg* of pincer movements had been assumed to leave the victor with considerable numbers of prisoners, and a certain amount of paper work for their reception had been done well in advance, it had always been envi-saged that it would be possible to keep these POWs in the East (Poland or Russia itself) and supply them from local resources. However, the Soviet scorched earth policy made this always difficult and often impossible.

It would almost seem as if, although the estimate was that a successful *blitzkrieg* against Russia would result in two to three million prisoners being taken within a short space of time, no one had taken the next logical step of instructing the Q branch to be prepared to supply food, fuel and building materials so much in excess of what normal procedure (divisional POW cages etc) anticipated. The POW Section of the War Ministry had been instructed to recruit staffs for 25 camps, each capable of accommodating upwards of 40 000 prisoners, but that appears to have been the extent of the actual preparations that were made, with the result that, as Generaloberst Jodl reported, the mortality rate was tragically high:

'The encircled Russian armies put up a fanatical resistance even though for the final eight or ten days they were without food supplies, so that they literally lived off tree-bark and roots, for they had withdrawn into the most inaccessible parts of the forests; thus, when they fell into our hands they were in such a state as to be scarcely able to move. It was impossible to march them away. The railway network having been destroyed, our own supply resources were strained, so it was impossible to transport them all away. There was no accommodation in the vicinity, immediate careful hospital treatment would have saved most of them. Rain set in almost at once and then came the cold, and that is why such a large proportion of just these prisoners from Wjasma perished.

That picture is elaborated by two reports from army quartermasters. The quartermaster of Army Group Mitte, wrote:

'Now as before, the most difficult problem is that of how to provision the multitude of POWs assembled in this area. This cannot possibly be done from army services alone. The camps themselves do not have either the equipment or the administration to feed such huge numbers. A camp with 20,000 POWs must cook ten tons of potatoes alone each day. This is impossible, because there is not enough cooking equipment. To obtain the provisions needed each day in the camp is itself not possible because there is not the transport. To use troops from the Transport Companies is impossible, since every available vehicle is required for stock-piling winter supplies for the troops. For this reason, too, only a minimal store of winter provisions for the camps has so far been acquired . . .'

Again, the quartermaster of Army Command 17 reported:

'In no single case has it been possible to provide the rations laid down. Fat, cheese, soya flour, jam and tea could not always be supplied even to our own troops. Millet, maize, sunflower seeds, buckwheat, lentils, peas and to some extent bread have had to be substituted.

Full or partial provision of the rations laid-down has proved simply impossible, because the rations were not obtainable. The prisoners could only be fed on what could be obtained locally. Preparation of their food itself presented difficulties, because only in very few cases did they have field kitchens with them. Even our own troops had to live off the land, because of difficulties in obtaining supplies. For some considerable time their rations even had to be halved.'

Dr Faulhaber, a steel-master sent to the Ukraine in the middle of October 1941, has described an encounter with Soviet POWs:

'The prisoners passed in seemingly endless columns. One of these consisted of 12,500 guarded by only thirty soldiers. Those who were unable to continue, were shot. We spent the night in a small village, where we had got bogged down in the mud. There was a transit camp there and we were witnesses of how at night the prisoners roasted and ate those of their fellows, whom our patrols had had to shoot for breaches of discipline.'

One hundred and twenty-nine years earlier, in this same part of the world other horrified witnesses had watched French soldiers, no longer combatants though perhaps not yet formally prisoners of war, eating their comrades who had died on Napoleon's great retreat out of Russia.

These glimpses of conditions on the Eastern Front show how little the victor's dilemma has changed since the days of Alexander the Great. In the great battle of Vjasma and Brjansk the Germans took twice as many prisoners as Alexander the Great did at Plateia, but despite the fact that Soviet Russia was not a signatory to the Geneva Convention and the Nazi philosophy was that Russians were inferior beings and as such not entitled to the

The American Civil War
is another particularly
gloomy chapter in the
history of the POW.
Rations are issued
(above) at Andersonville
Prison on August 17,
1864 and (right)
Confederate prisoners
captured in the
Shenandoah Valley
under guard in a Union
camp, May 1862.

same treatment as, say, French or British prisoners, the Germans could not adopt Alexander's drastic solution of slaughter. Their dilemma was how to provide even the most elementary accommodation for 662 000 men, the population of a city the size of Manchester. 'The evacuation of prisoners of war', Colonel J K Daly of the US Corps of Military Police wrote from personal experience 'is one of the functions which normally is taken for granted, like the supply of food and water, and seldom is mentioned unless something goes wrong.' And things frequently seem to go wrong. Indeed, the real surprise is that they ever go right when one considers the numbers of men needed to guard and transport large numbers of prisoners, let alone the huge quantities of food, water, fuel etc needed.

POW LOGISTICS AND D-DAY

Before the Normandy landing, the Allies were able to plan the evacuation and dispersal of the prisoners they knew they were going to take. As a result the US Theater Provost Marshal, for example, was told that he should prepare to deal with 25 000–50 000 prisoners. In fact the number was 30 000, who had to be guarded and transported from the collecting points to a reception centre and taken to distribution centres, from which they were shipped to ports in the USA and then sent to various base camps. (In comparing the tasks and the difficulties of the Allies in France and Germany and of the Germans in Russia, it is irrelevant that the Germans had planned *not* to send any prisoners back to Germany, but to retain them all in Poland or Russia, where they were to be fed and housed off the land which they were to till and re-establish. They still had to be distributed over perhaps even greater distances, always into a more-or-less ravaged area.)

In Normandy, the Americans collected the prisoners from the various Divisions using two-and-a-half ton trucks, which would accommodate 60 men at a time. Each truck was guarded by three Rangers: one sitting in the cab, beside the driver, watching the truck in front; the other two sat, one on each mudguard, facing backwards, watching the truck on which they rode. The whole column was headed by a Ranger on a motorcycle and brought up by two more in a quarter–ton truck. On arrival at the reception enclosure (built by the First Army Engineers), those who were wounded or ill were sent for medical treatment and the others segregated according to arm (Reichswehr, SS, Luftwaffe, etc) rank and nationality before being moved in groups to one or other of the several enclosures built along the beaches between Foucarville and Formigny, which were all well stocked with rations. Here, they were briefly interrogated, listed and so shipped to England, where they were disembarked into a Reception Enclosure and taken to a Distribution Enclosure, where they were questioned, searched, disinfected, fed and given any necessary medical attention or clothing. They were next sent to an Evacuation Enclosure and then by sea to the United States.

To achieve all this there were three Military Police POW Processing Companies, each of three platoons of 34 men, one platoon being assigned to each of the eight Evacuation Enclosures with the remaining one held in reserve and sent to wherever demand was highest. These platoons sifted through the prisoners separating nationalities, ranks, arms and so on. Then there were 19 Military Police Escort Guard Companies totalling 137 men. Three of these companies were allocated to the Engineers to operate their Beach Enclosures; three were allocated to the Reception Enclosure in England: one to guard the enclosure itself, one to guard the ships and boats bringing the prisoners from France and one to guard the four trains that ran

Overleaf: German prisoners taken by US forces being disembarked at a distribution centre. The guards will have been provided by one of the US Military Police Companies.

Tents are the easiest and quickest means of providing shelter for prisoners in large numbers. This camp with its walkways, looks better than most were, but whatever the type of camp there are problems of drainage, sanitation, water supply and cooking facilities that are seldom easy to solve.

daily to the Distribution Enclosure, which was itself run and the trains from it to the Evacuation Enclosure guarded by a further three companies. Three other companies were allocated to the Advanced Section, Communications Zone, and one was distributed among the ports on the south coast to take charge of odd batches of prisoners that might turn up there. In addition 21 Military Police Companies were set up for the 'zone of the interior' for the reception and guarding of POWs at Evacuation Enclosures and to act as guards on ships and boats, and on trains between ports of disembarkation and POW base camps in the USA.

Thus in all some 2700 men were engaged in dealing, as far as possible in accordance with the Geneva Convention, with 30 000 POWs, a ratio of 11 to one. The whole operation had been most carefully planned and worked out. All the installations in England had been prepared in advance and were manned and ready to operate by D-Day. It was a triumph of planning and coordination. But, once the Allies had penetrated inland, improvization had to some extent to replace planning. There was still a proper and effective organization for looking after POWs. The US 106th Infantry Division, which had been mauled in the Ardennes, was given the task of guarding the POWs taken by the US Fifteenth Army. At one point it was dealing with 920 000 POWs, its own strength then being 40 000, a ratio of one to 23; though, as far from all the 40 000 were available for guard duty, the ratio here was nearer to one to 100 or one to 150. They had to deal with men of at least 18 different nationalities (many of whom could not understand German!), of all ranks and shades of political opinion, of both sexes and all ages from boys of seven to men of 80.

Thus, even the mighty US army with all its forward planning and vast resources, sometimes found extreme difficulty in securing and transporting

When in the field, not even the most scrupulous about personal hygiene can keep themselves clean. As a result, prisoners, especially those taken at the end of a lengthy battle, have to be deloused. These prisoners are being sprayed with a louse-killing liquid to protect them (and others) until they can be properly bathed and provided with clean clothes.

the vast quantities of rations, fuel, medical supplies and cooking facilities needed for close on a million POWs, as well as all that was required by the five field armies driving forward east of the Rhine. Indeed, the difficulties in supplying forward troops were such that captured enemy stores that would otherwise have been available to supply the POWs, had to be command-eered and used by the Allies as they advanced. The 106th Division had to be given a further 135 two-and-a-half–ton trucks to enable it to do its job. Even so, at one point there was an almost total lack of medical supplies (tents, blankets, stretchers, etc), though, when the five Field Hospitals attached to the Division got going, there were beds for 23 000 within the POW enclo-sures and a further 16 000 available in the Field Hospitals, so that there was accommodation for three to four per cent of the POW population.

Prisoners were to be brought from the Divisions into enclosures, con-sisting of a double barbed wire perimeter fence, the two fences being 10 ft (2.9m) apart and the intervening space filled with concertina wire. There were to be guard towers, box latrines and an access road, though no interior roads. These enclosures were to be built by the army Engineers, who also had to lay on a supply of water, one tap per kitchen for drinking and cooking, estimated at one gallon per man per day, while extra water would also be needed for washing. Electricity was needed to light at least the perimeter fence. The prisoners themselves were to supply the labour for digging latrines, building food stores, shelters, etc. Water was always a major diffi-culty. One of the larger enclosures was so full that it needed 150 000 gallons a day. which, initially, had to be brought in five-gallon cans. Fuel (wood and coal) for cooking was another difficulty, 106th Division having to collect and distribute 400 tons a day. Difficulties, as always, increased with the length of the supply line. The area served by 106th Division was at one time 340 road

A glint of sunlight and a large river give these Russians captured by the Austrians on the Isonzo during World War I an opportunity to clean both body and clothes. The absence of such facilities was one of the more irksome of the deprivations experienced in so many officers' camps.

Overleaf: A dejected group of Japanese prisoners captured by troops of 7th Infantry Division on Okinawa. They will soon be searched by the military police in the background.

miles along the Rhine and 600 miles deep.

Despite all the resources available and all the careful planning and organization of them, in the final phase of the war, some of the enclosures for the reception of prisoners consisted:

'only of areas of ground surrounded by a single barbed wire fence. Most were completely destitute of shelter of any description except for scraps of canvas, boards or tin. Guard towers were absent at most places. The water supply into the enclosures had either not yet been completed or was completely inadequate. An enclosure at Remagen, designed ultimately to accommodate 100 000 prisoners had been only half completed and was occupied by double its capacity. Ten thousand prisoners of war were on sick report at this enclosure . . . Roads leading to the enclosure in all directions were clogged with truck convoys filled with prisoners sent to the rear by the Ninth United States Army, in charge of the Military Police of at least nine different divisions. Seven trains of prisoners were reported east of the Rhine awaiting an opportunity to cross the only bridge. During the first afternoon of the occupancy of this camp, which was far from being complete, a total of 35 000 prisoners were counted through the gates . . . Food and medical supplies were extremely short or completely absent. The weather was cold and rainy . . .'

So Major-General D A Stroh, former commander of 106th Infantry Division, writing in 1946. But that does not complete the list of their difficulties.

When a position is surrounded and the enemy surrenders, he will have with him his field kitchen or other equipment for cooking and washing. On a

planned withdrawal with ample time allowed, a unit will be able to take its kitchen equipment with it, but when the retreat is rapid and perhaps made with little or no notice, this may not be possible; it certainly was not possible for the Germans sent to 106th Infantry Division, most of whom had no individual cooking equipment, any more than the surrendering Russians who emerged out of the forests on the Eastern Front; nor indeed, did they have anything heavier, such as a field kitchen, for communal use.

A quick search by the Division produced a number of 200-gallon (9 hectol) boilers, each capable of feeding a thousand men, but most of these boilers were designed to burn oil or electricity and had to be converted to wood or coal before they could be used. Nor was there ever enough of them and much had to be improvized. Empty oil drums were pressed into service and at one enclosure an old steam locomotive was run in on an improvized track to provide steam for the cooking boiler. Such a lack of cooking facilities made it imperative to have rations that did not require cooking. This was a further difficulty, as most rations contained flour and lard, which had to be

Germans surrendering at Cherbourg, 1944. Many of them still have considerable personal possessions and may well have enough for all their immediate needs except shelter. It is the number of them that presents the problem.

removed. Later the flour was taken to local civilian bakeries which were ordered to bake bread for the POWs and this helped to relieve the situation. Two weeks and more after capture, the food distribution points had only one day's rations in hand, while the individual enclosures did not even have that much.

Nobody can be blamed for these situations. With the best will in the world, it is often physically impossible to give POWs the treatment required by the Geneva Convention. Circumstances over which the captor has no real control make it impossible to avoid distress and suffering in the short term. Between conditions on the Western Front in 1944 and on the Eastern Front in 1942 the only real difference was one of degree.

Once accommodated, the well being of prisoners depended very largely on discipline, without which demoralization set in. In officers' camps internal discipline was provided and administered by the prisoners themselves. George Putnam, who was himself a prisoner in Virginia in 1854–5, writing of his experiences, said:

A prisoner being thoroughly searched before entering the POW cage.

The unsung heroes of the Red Cross

Each country's own Red Cross Society either independently or with a sister organization, as in Great Britain, with the Order of St John of Jerusalem, organized the packing and despatch of parcels of up to 10 lbs of clothing and comforts that next of kin can send each POW once every three months. It also sent, each POW a parcel of ten shillings worth of food each week, though these were not necessarilly received as regularly, being often delayed by ill will, inefficiency or physical difficulties (bombing of railways, bridges, roads etc.)

The International Red Cross receives requisitions for special medicines, drugs, invalid foods, spectacles, disinfectants etc direct from camp doctors and supplies them direct. Those who go blind are sent Braille textbooks, watches, typewriters etc. The needs of the deaf are similarly looked after.

The minds of POWs are equally well considered: books are supplied on all subjects from accoutancy to zoology. In World War II thousands of study courses were prepared with university help and the necessary texts supplied. (British POWs were sent 86000 books in the first three years). Musical instruments are costly and difficult to obtain, but many have been sent and provided a more effective therapy than many other aspects of Red Cross help, which has included equipment for playing football, base-ball etc as well as playing cards, draughts, backgammon, halma, chess, monopoly, mahjong and more.

Allied POWs in Europe were sent 20 million standard Red Cross food parcels from the UK alone in World War II (Indian troops were sent special food). New Zealand sent 6000–8000 parcels a week, Canada and Australia together 80000 a week. South Africa had transport difficulties and contributed money instead.

At the same time the American Red Cross was being as or more generous in the help it sent to POWs.

The work entailed in organizing, buying, packing, despatching, transporting, recording all these many tons of food and comforts was mostly done by unpaid volunteers. Some devoted all their time, others as much as other essential work left them, to this great humanitarian and patriotic task.

There has been no war since 1929 in which the Red Cross has not won the right to 'battle honours', and few POWs who do not owe a debt of gratitude, if nothing more, to this organization.

George Putnam refers to the danger to the individual prisoner of war of mental stagnation developing into idiocy and thus inflicting more disastrous damage than physical deprivation can. Once the fighting is over the sanity of countless thousands of POWs in their camps has been saved by the Red Cross supplying books, music and musical instruments, games, sports equipment, theatrical equipment, even complete courses of study; at the same time as the Red Cross food parcels and special medicines have saved more lives than have been lost on the battlefield.

The heart of this mighty humanitarian effort is the International Red Cross working from Geneva and serving both sides impartially. It appoints delegates who visit POW camps monitoring the treatment of POWs and the conditions of their detention. Of these delegates in World War II ten lost their lives in the course of their duties. What POWs have appreciated most, has been the distribution of letters from home to POWs and those from POWs to their homes. In World War II more than 120 million such letters and 36 million parcels were distributed via the Red Cross.

Wounded prisoners of World War I and II could expect fairly swift attention for their wounds. This is a scene at a Field Dressing Station in World War I.

'I have referred to the "government" of the prison — and the fact that we accepted, at least in our officers' prison, the authority of seniors just as we should have done in camp. I believe that this acceptance of authority and maintenance of discipline accounted for the better success on the part of officers as compared with the enlisted men in maintaining the vitality and in lessening the percentage of illness and death. There were two other prisons in the town, both I believe tobacco warehouses, in which enlisted men were confined, possibly a thousand or more. There was no difference in the quarters and no difference in the food between the prisons; but we understood from the Confederate sergeants that the percentage of deaths among the men were much greater than among the officers.'

MEDICINE UNDER STRESS

Putnam refers to medical care being the worst lack of all and this understandably has always been so. When a country goes to war, increasing the size of its army, it inevitably deprives the civilian population of some of its doctors, so that when prisoners arrive in any number and require medical care the civilian population must be further deprived to look after the POWs. These doctors, trying to deal with an excessive number of patients, find that they often cannot even understand them. This had in the past led to an appalling situation when doctors, unable to cope, have been tempted to let an epidemic spread and so rid them of a burden, and have even assisted in spreading the epidemic, by having infected patients transferred from one camp to another. (This has, in fact, been documented from Roumania and Russia in World War 1.) Neither doctors nor medicines, even wonder drugs and antibiotics, can be produced on demand at all times, so that today such a situation might easily arise again.

Modern regulations require the POW to be clothed and shod by the detaining power, but previously this was considered too great a burden and countries were expected to provide clothes for their own captive soldiers.

This question of clothing for POWs has always been a problem. POWs seldom have any possessions of their own. They may have been captured in a hot climate and sent to captivity in a cold one; in addition, there are countless cases of POWs selling clothing to obtain food on the march to their place of confinement, because the captors' own organization had broken down and they were starving. This sort of thing is well documented from the American Civil War, and from Russia during World Wars I and II and in the Far East. At their destination ORs will probably be put to work and this further wears out their clothing. In time of war, clothing has always been difficult to replace, especially from the resources of the smaller countries. Lack of raw materials and trading difficulties may make it impossible. Even in tropical climates, where under normal conditions nakedness would be perfectly tolerable, the European needs some clothing as protection from the worst of the sun. The supply of adequate clothing can be a problem, and it is now regarded as the duty of the detaining power to provide NCOs and ORs with it. Officers provide their own. In March 1915 there were 654 173 POWs in Germany; by August the number had grown to 1 115 926 and by October the total was 2 526 922. The number of civilians required to make even the most elementary clothing for such a number would be considerable indeed and it would never have been supplied without the parcels sent out from home via the Red Cross.

Conditions in camps varied. These variations were sometimes due to local conditions: difficulties of supply, transport, etc, sometimes to the temperament of those in charge of the camps. Apart from the inadequacies of the food, except where generously supplemented by Red Cross parcels, most irksome seems to have been the difficulty of keeping body and clothes clean. This and the often inadequate latrine arrangements are recurring themes in many POWs' diaries. One diary records a notable day when the laundry was returned after a long delay and the diarist discovered that his garments had been mended.

Letters were an important factor in maintaining POWs' spirits. There were difficulties here, not surprisingly. It must be remembered that there were vast numbers of letters, cards and parcels involved and a mammoth task in distributing them. In the First World War in April 1918, the Swiss Post Office transmitted 12 441 211 letters and cards, 3 549 523 parcels and 133 852 money orders.

Barbed wire was invented in 1873 and this made it possible to erect more or less escape-proof fences round tented or other primitive accommodation comparatively quickly, so that the standard of initial accommodation tended to go down if anything, but the effect of other modern inventions has been to improve it. As T J Walker has put it:

> 'The consideration of the prison life of our captives at the close of the 18th century will serve to accentuate the difference between their surroundings, their life and their fate, and that of the prisoners taken a hundred years later by either side in the South African War; and the picture of the French and Dutch prisoners in the hulks or even in the depots in 1800, contrasted with that of the Boers in St Helena and Ceylon in 1900, must fill us with thankfulness for what the centuries advance in humanity . . .
>
> In 1900 steam navigation, telegraphic communications and Britain's command of the sea made it possible for her to place her prisoners hors de combat in islands whence escape was impossible and where conditions of life were comparatively comfortable . . .

Another way of minimizing the amount of surveillance of POWs was the system of granting parole, whereby, in return for an undertaking, usually an oath given in writing, not to try to escape or to take any further part in hostilities or do anything injurious to the interests of your enemy, you were allowed to live in private accommodation among the civilian population or even to go home. This system started in the days when ransoms were normally paid and people normally kept their word, and it continued until World War I, though now that officers were generally considered morally bound to try to escape, the system has no further application. It is interesting that, despite all that has been written about the Oriental attitude to surrender and the prisoner of war, parole was granted by the Japanese to Russian officers who surrendered at Port Arthur. This applied also to freedom to take exercise in various ways within given areas. Those on parole were not allowed to carry a weapon, nor to send or receive letters or telephone calls while they were out, nor to visit others in civilian accommodation without special permission. They were, however, allowed to live with their wives and families, though this required special sanction. What a very different attitude this was to that of the Japanese command in World War II!

Thirty-five years later, lack of communications, along with other factors, could still make barbed wire and guards unnecessary. In the Soviet colonies, such as Kazahkstan, distances are so huge that a POW who escaped from his place of confinement would die of starvation before he reached another human dwelling from which to beg or steal. In his book about Korea, *The Wooden Boxes*, D G Kinne has described how he and his fellows came to a POW camp where there was no barbed wire, no encircling fence, no machine-gun trained inwards, and how they eventually realized that none of these were needed, for the simple reason that the POWs were so enfeebled by the poverty of their diet and the lack of medical supplies that they had no earthly chance.

CAMPS OF ALL SIZES

In World War II no one expected captivity to last long and there was an element of temporariness about all the accommodation provided for POWs. One French officer captured in the first onslaught has described his arrival at an Oflag in distant Pomerania and the camp itself:

'At four o'clock in the morning, the train stopped. Outside we could hear hoarse shouts and the tread of boots on the embankment. The vans were unlocked. In the first pale light of dawn, a thousand French officers suddenly found themselves in open country, in the depths of Pomerania. Dreary wastes of sand and fields of potatoes stretched for miles all round them. "Do you see? Do you see?" shouted Dubreuil. We all instinctively looked in the same direction, and were spellbound by the most fantastic sight. Though at first we couldn't quite make out what it was, we guessed subconsciously. About 600 yards away, where the plain joined the pine-wood, a kind of opera-stage-setting loomed up, floodlit, and looking like something between an African village and a fortified casino — a fantastic jumble of vast barbed wire enclosures, huts and sentry-boxes. That's where we were being taken. There, at the edge of the wood, the stage stood ready for us, the actors . . .

'This was the cage in which Hitler was imprisoning us . . . The fortress round the camp was a huge network of barbed wire in two rows, about 7 feet high and 6 feet apart. The space between the two rows was filled with a vast tangle of springy wire, like thick underbrush with iron thorns. At every 200 feet or so there were sentry-posts about 60 feet high, bristling with bren-guns and fitted up with searchlights. Inside the enclosure there was no black-out, and no night. From dusk till dawn the camp was illuminated as brilliantly as a circus ring. So for four years the German darkness has been lit by thirty or forty pools of light . . .

'The Oflag was divided by barbed wire into four distinct compartments called "Blocks". Each block consisted of anything from twelve to twenty huts, spaced out in two rows or formed in a circle round the communal latrine or *Abort*.

'A little way off was Block 5 — as the cemetery was called.

'The living-quarters were wooden huts where three layers of men slept in three-decker wooden bunks. When one wanted to go to bed, one would have to crawl into a bunk on all fours, like a dog getting into its kennel, unless one were lucky enough to have a top bunk in which case one only needed to hoist oneself up. When we were all in our bunks, anyone coming into the room in the middle of the night and seeing these layers of bodies would have thought he had walked into a mortuary.'

Another camp to which mostly British officers were sent was the old fortress Thorn or Torun, in Poland. John Mansell and his fellow POWs arrived there in March 1941:

'The moment the train stopped it was obvious that we were in for trouble. Arc lights and the headlights of army cars, full on, lit up the station yard — it was strange to see undimmed headlights again. These lights threw into silhouette the welcoming party — a row of guards, their rifles at the ready, safety catches off and fingers on triggers, and a further group with tommy guns — rather jolly!. . .

'Eventually we marched off along an appallingly muddy track — apparently typical Poland — past various forts, for about half a mile and then we were pitched into Hollywood. After that train journey, it was great to arrive at our destination, whatever its appearance might have been. But this exceeded all expectations. It all happened so suddenly and we were inside so quickly, that there was little time for a clear picture — I merely had a jumbled vision first of a high brick wall and massive gates, of wire and iron rails, of a bridge over a chasm (which we later found to be a dry moat) and the prison-like entrance to whatever sort of building it was. All this was made particularly vivid as the scene was lit by powerful arc lights, making even blacker whatever lay on either side. Well, we were across this bridge in no time and through the arched entrance to the fort, as it proved to be, into a wide arched corridor, about 15 feet wide and 150 feet long, which brought to my mind a thoroughfare in an Underground Goods Station in London. It was well lit and standing at the top of it, for it was an appreciable slope, we were met by presumably the Kommandant and his staff.

'Our hosts now showed us to our rooms! We were numbered off — first of all the Brigadier and Colonels for one room, then the Majors (no longer termed senior officers with the Brigadier here), then the remainder by 16's. We retraced our steps back down the tube station and then through some heavily barred gates and down to what we imagined from the upper level to be dungeons, to what in actual fact proved to be the ground floor at moat level . . .

'Our room is No 8. It is about 30 feet by 16 feet with a small bay in the middle of one side which takes 2 beds (4 people) and a stove in the middle of the other side of the typical German and extremely efficient pattern. Over the stove is the only store in the room, formed by the brickwork over two recesses in the walls on either side of the stove. These recesses have their purposes after 8 pm and before 7.30 am, between which hours the rooms are locked (a punitive measure imposed because some German POWs in Canada were understood to be having their rooms locked in this way). In them are housed 3 buckets which serve all purposes. On the other side there are 2 buckets, on the other a broom and a bucket — in the latter the food basins are washed up. As this is the only pail in the room it is difficult to prevent some from using it for shaving water. There are 2 windows — or rather $1\frac{1}{4}$ — the big one about 5 foot x 4 foot, the small about 3 foot 6 inches x 9 inches in the centre, 6 inches at the sides as they are arched. Both windows are barred but can be opened. The room had an arched ceiling and by day is very dark. There are 2 tables in the centre of the room — each about 5 foot by 2 foot 6 inches. The floor is — thank God — wooden boarded. The beds themselves are double-decker with straw-filled (or rather wood-shaving filled) palliasses which have no covers. On them we found 2 blankets and a small towel. . . . We each have a china bowl and a spoon and a small cup.

'Immediately after supper, feeling much better, the next thing was a wash. Our (British) orderly (1 to each room) told us not to drink the water for fear of diphtheria — 200 had died last summer — but that it is all right to brush one's teeth with it. All the water in the fort has to be pumped up by hand, so there isn't much. There is a party on the pump all day . . .

'There is a crowd of 30 chaps round a long trough. A $\frac{1}{2}$-inch pipe runs along the top of this and out of it a trickle of water drops from about 8 holes punctured at intervals along it. This place might well be a dungeon. Everyone is laughing like hell — the whole scene is really pretty comic. Before we are locked up there is one more place to visit — and let's make it a really satisfactory visit as we've got to last out a long time! — the latrine. This proved to be the most fantastic of all our "views" of the Castle yet. In the centre was what was later to become known as "the Cruet". This is formed by a central vertical drainpipe and clustered round it about 5 three-cornered compartments with wooden dividing partitions all radiating from the centre, each with a wooden seat with a hole in it and a tin lid. The one outside wall has 2 musket slits in it; the other two the devices for the operation termed since nursery days, No 1. These could only be described by picture — in other words they are indescribable.

'Getting into bed was rather tricky, on the upper bunks — because they are so infernally high . . . Actually I slept like a log, much too tired to move, but woke at 7.30 feeling intensely cold and almost off my bed . . . The turning of the key before going to sleep really did make one feel one was a criminal and that the tumbril would be calling in the morning . . .

'The chapel is worth sketching — another underground cul-de-sac — brick-built and from the austere point of view, thoroughly dramatic — in fact what I have always visualized as a prison chapel. Wooden rickety benches to sit on — extremely cold, but the driest room I have seen yet. It is a curious coincidence that we should have arrived here almost the 1st day of Lent — we have certainly given up enough!. . .

'I had a walk on Mappin Terrace this morning. There is nothing to see here except the sky and the surrounding earthworks which camouflage the fort, with sentries, barbed wire and machine-gun to keep us in. A foot on the bank and the sentries have orders to shoot without warning.'

ORIENTAL POWS AND INHUMAN CONDITIONS

On the other side of the world not only was the attitude to the POW utterly different, but the treatment he received and the conditions in which he lived were very different too. It may be that the Japanese were prepared, if need be, to make their own men work and live in such conditions as they imposed on the Allied POWs, but this has yet to be substantiated. The fact remains that Allied POWs in Japanese and later Korean and Vietnamese hands, suffered as much or perhaps more than the most unfortunate prisoner of mediaeval times or of those in Soviet camps. Russell Braddon has thus described one camp in which he was imprisoned:

'River Valley Camp lay on either side of an especially foul little stream from which we were in the habit of fishing frogs for the purpose of conducting frog races and gambling thereon. This gambling was quickly forbidden by the authorities — which ban we habitually ignored, our $3 monthly pay check having by this time been rendered valueless by inflation.

'Apart from the frogs and the foul stream, there were rows upon rows of dilapidated attap huts with two tiers of bamboo decking running down each side of a mud passageway. On each of these slept hundreds of men, whilst in the bamboo supports and decks and the attap roofing there lurked many billions of bugs — all of them with Anglophobia.

'And as well as the huts and the bugs there was masses of mud — which mud the English troops on the far side of the stream declared to be more villainous in their area, whilst we asserted that it was worse in ours. Over the whole joyful scene hung the clouds of depression caused by evilly-disposed guards — Japs who bashed and Sikhs who, given the smallest chance, would rape . . .

'Our work lay in the docks of Singapore's Kepple Harbour — in the go-downs . . . we lugged bombs *from the go-downs up the gang plank and down into the holds of ships bound for the Pacific Islands. Though the 500-lb bombs were obviously beyond the powers of one man, the Nips would not compromise over the 250-pounders. One man one bomb it was. And for day after day, anything up to sixteen hours a day, we staggered under the weight of these bombs in their crude deal crates. They tore the skin and flesh on one's shoulders and the bashings were incessant. For the second time in my career I found myself thinking of a most unsavoury abode as "home", and towards the end of a day's violence, I would long for the mud and the bugs of River Valley.'

Temperament has a lot to do with the way in which individuals, even with the same background will react to similar sets of circumstances. Another prisoner in River Valley Camp was Ian Scott, a member of the Chartered Bank of India and a corporal in the Singapore Volunteer Defence Force. He kept a journal (which has never been published) in which he recorded the day's events and his reactions to them — at the time, not written up in retrospect. He was fortunate, if anyone in captivity can be called fortunate, for in his journal for May 1942 he describes life in Changi thus:

'What did we have to do at Changi? Jobs for our own health, feeding and comfort, which were distributed round the companies and platoons in rotation, but due to a large percentage of sick (caused by change of diet and lack of nutrition) the fit got more and more to do. The 'fatigues' were chiefly in the morning from 10 to 12.30, but sometimes had to be done in the afternoon also. The jobs were wood-cutting, chopping and collecting: until the water system was repaired, drawing water from the well and carrying it to the cookhouse; collecting rations and grinding rice for flour; digging pits for latrines, digging anti-malarial drains in a marshy area: going to the sea and collecting sea-water to be evaporated into salt, to augment our meagre salt ration. Duties of mess orderlies for cleaning up after meals and bringing the food from the cookhouse, barrack-room orderlies for sweeping, etc etc. It all filled in our time and some of them proved very strenuous, especially on our scant rice diet. In our spare time we played Bridge . . . The carrier platoon ran a library for the 1st Battalion and had about 200/300 books and nearly always I had one to go on with.'

Then they were moved to Singapore and housed in huts built by the British as huts for evacuees, but never used. These were 200 ft long and 30 ft wide

Overleaf: American prisoners in a Japanese camp (on Bataan, Corregidor) sometime during 1941–2. Food — that major preoccupation of the POW — is apparently uppermost in the minds of these captives.

*According to the international convention, to which Japan did not subscribe, POWs were not to be made to work making or handling munitions or anything that might harm their own side.

with a gangway of earth down the middle, on each side of which were two stories of boarding as beds. On these each of 250 men had two-and-a-half feet of space:

'We have rigged up many clothes lines and impromptu boards as shelves and hooks and wires suspend all sorts of clothing from the roof. The inside of the hut always looks like a kitchen on a wet washing day or an old junk shop.'

A POWERFUL CONTRAST

Moved to a camp near the Thailand frontier, Ian Scott's fellow prisoners continued the amateur theatricals they had begun at Changi, of which his journal records:

'The whole cast had put in very hard work in rehearsal from 8.30 pm to midnight each evening for a week or two and all after a hard day's manual labour. They deserved the fried eggs and rice fritters they got after each night's show and on the last night a "binge" when a bottle of samsu (rice wine) was presented by the Nip Commandant and some of our officers. The Nip Commandant joined in the fun and encouraged the fellows to hold more concerts. He told them that he felt quite disappointed that he might miss the next show, for he had been warned that he might be required to report up river on duty. He chatted with Daryl and the lads and passed round his cigarettes (which, of course, were not made of "jungle weed") and he insisted that "the girls" sit beside him and plied them with samsu. No wonder some were horribly "lit" and had terrific hangovers, but matters were put right as the concert party were given a holiday the following day. We are lucky in having such a good Nip in charge of the camp and he does try and make our life as easy as possible, for the camp is considered the best on the river (Kwai) — and there are supposed to be 17,000 British POWs hereabouts. The other camps have very severe restrictions — no smoking, no camp fires and not allowed outside the huts after 10 pm. I believe our food and conditions are better and consequently our health and spirits are much better.'

Later again, after a spell in the camp hospital:
1.2.44.

'I came out of hospital to the convalescent ward about the 15th November and have kept reasonably fit. I have put on a considerable amount of weight (weight I had lost) but I expect I am a good bit under my peacetime normal. For months I have had sores — suppurating ones on hands, feet, bottom and shoulders, which have been extremely sore at times. It has also been difficult to lie down or to wear things on one's feet, but, thank goodness, they are at last clearing up. Persistent hot water to scrub them clean and, when available, a variety of medicines have been my treatment. It is a blood disorder due to vitamin deficiency and nearly everyone has had a dose of these sores. I have been feeling pretty well due to an extremely lucky "bolt from the blue". A large sum (for these days) of cash came into camp secretly for members of the Chartered Bank in the vicinity — from where and how is a mystery and it is safest to make few enquiries and the least said the better, for stories get around. So we just count our blessings . . . By this I can augment my meals for about 8 to 10 months to a standard comparable to what an officer can do, who gets a monthly salary whether they are working or not. Now I spend about 50 stgs to 70 stgs and buy eggs, meat, sugar, fish, limes, bananas, coconut oil or pork fat. Even special cakes on sale in the afternoons — of course not all on the same day. Here is the current price list . . .

'The Nips now, besides holding roll-call after breakfast and evening meal, as has always been done, go round the huts at night — two or three times each night — and check up the numbers of personnel to see none are missing. For it has been quite common practice for chaps being outside camp on "business". Some chaps still go out for various purposes, bringing in contraband (as far as Nips are concerned) and to purchase same they sell watches and such like. On Xmas night two fellows were not present at the check up during the night and were caught and punished quite justly by the Nips, but on New Year's Eve a roll-call was held just 10 minutes after lights-out and one man from this hut was found missing. Next morning it was learned he was dead — shot by the Nips. He had not been outside but was on his way back to this hut about 11.10 pm (ten minutes late certainly) and had been spotted by the Nips near the outside fence, for the hut he had been visiting was near the fence — and without any further questioning he was taken and shot. But I think, and we all do, that there was no justice and the penalty was too severe . . . The Yellow Bastards!'

Compare these conditions with those in Kilimatinde Camp in German East Africa 26 years earlier and 4500 miles away. Admittedly this was World War I, when war had not yet become 'total' again, as it had been in antiquity, but the differences are so enormous that there is really no comparison between the conditions in Singapore and those in Kilimatinde, as described by Charles Miller in *Battle for the Bundu*:

'. . . most of the military prisoners were housed at a village called Milimatinde, some miles down the Central railway . . . At Kilimatinde (Buttermilk Mill), our camp commandant greeted each newly-arrived POW with a grim recital of draconian rules, followed by a personal handshake. Going to their quarters, the prisoners found beds, dressers, cane chairs, wash-stands and basins — all kept tidy by African servants. Before food began to run out, meals were plain but ample, consisting mainly of meat, bread, cheese; and served by African waiters in a roomy mess hall. The prison cook was a hausfrau whose habit of boiling all meat caused continual complaints; she also touched off a wave of consternation among the British prisoners by making a Christmas pudding in cold slices. Tea (or rather coffee or milk) was served punctually at four o'clock every afternoon, although for one period the commandant had the ritual suspended to punish the prisoners for cheering. . . .

But forward again to the Korean War of 1950–53; conditions in 'Death Valley' were described thus:

'Death Valley was divided into two sections, north and south, about two miles apart. The officers were in the south section with approximately 1000 prisoners. The north section was approximately half that size. In the south section there were six barrack-like buildings with four to six units per barracks. A unit consisted of a room and a kitchen area. There were 24 men in Captain X's unit — so crowded that two-thirds of them had to sit with their knees under their chins, while the remaining one-third would lie down. The men rotated positions. Under-the-floor type

The cast of a play put on by Russians captured by Austrians in World War I. The staging of plays was a favourite form of escapism for prisoners of both world wars. Quite often some of the actors were professionals

Laughter and forgetting — entertainment and the POW

There were no ENSA parties to entertain POWs and they had to provide their own amusement. The larger camps were able to produce enough talent — some of it amateur, some professional — to put on plays, stage musicals, and give concerts. Lectures and talks, which perhaps should be labelled education, also helped to pass the time. Books, too, were a tremendous solace for many.

Music can be a great solace and concerts, whether orchestral or choral, were a useful way of taking people's minds off the fact of their captivity. The listener is transported into a world of pure beauty without the element of make-believe inherent in the theatre.

of heating was used, but wood was so scarce that heat was available for only one hour each day. Food consisted of 400 grams of cracked corn per man per day.'

But it is above all the beatings, bashings, kicks, slashings, the deliberate torture that sets the Orientals' treatment of their prisoners apart and which makes it so incomprehensible to the Westerner. There has never been anything like it. The nearest equivalent, perhaps, would be the treatment meted out to the captives sent to the galleys of the Ottoman Empire and the Barbary pirates, but if they could have had the choice, most inmates of River Valley or Death Valley would have preferred to be chained to an oar.

The conditions under which POWs were kept has never been solely a matter of what is considered necessary to guard them, nor of what is available in the way of suitable accommodation and food judged by the relevant standards of East or West. Often conditions have been changed as a reprisal, on the tit-for-tat basis, which has been the main factor in assuring reasonably decent conditions for prisoners of war in the West since the Peninsular War.

In recent wars, the propaganda machines of the belligerents have played quite a part in dictating conditions in certain camps. The machine may have wanted photographs to show how well POWs were treated in that country and so a certain number were given especially good quarters and fed like fighting cocks until they could be photographed, healthy and well fed. On the other hand, when the propaganda machine was trying to compel POWs to sign peace petitions or confessions of guilt (for alleged use of gas or germ warfare) prisoners have been subjected to the most horrifying tortures, outdoing even those inflicted on the unfortunate POWs of the fifteenth and sixteenth centuries who were similarly maltreated to hasten payment of their ransoms. In the latter case, it was not a question of breaking their resistance, as it was with those whose signatures were wanted on a peace petition. A UK Ministry of Defence publication of 1955 has described some of the measures taken in Korea in the hope of breaking a man's resistance:

'For this purpose solitary confinement was sometimes sufficient in itself. This is hardly to be wondered at, for the conditions of this punishment were appalling. According to one of the victims, the "normal" treatment while in solitary confinement in camps was "to be made to stand or sit at attention (legs outstretched) from 04.30 hours to 23.00 hours daily." For the remainder of the day prisoners were allowed to sleep but were continually roused by the guard "to make sure they were still there". There were no beds and no bedding. Shoes and clothing, except for underclothes, were often denied, sometimes for months at a time, while visits to the latrine would be permitted only once or twice a day, even when the prisoner had dysentery. At Camp 1 the Chinese built a number of boxes about 5 ft by 3 ft by 2 ft for prisoners undergoing sentences of solitary confinement. In one of these one private of the Gloucesters spent just over six months. The food was appalling and often stopped for several days at a time. Water was inadequate and one prisoner, though he had three meals a day, received no soup, water or boiled food. This went on for eleven days and when he complained he was told that fluids were being withheld to help him with his "self-reflections".

'If the Chinese wanted results quickly this treatment was intensified, and beating in one form or another was fairly common. A corporal of the Gloucesters who refused to give any information at all to the

Chinese was taken out one evening at 9 o'clock at night and beaten by two Chinese until 3 o'clock in the morning with a club similar to a baseball bat. He had to stand to attention, stripped to the waist. At one point another Chinese came and took him down to the river and gave him a personal beating for some reason of his own. Prisoners were often bound with rope or wire for long periods; sometimes handcuffs were used. One British prisoner spent eight months in handcuffs, which were frequently tightened.

'In winter opportunities for torture increased. (POWs) are known to have been marched barefooted onto the frozen Yalu river where water was poured over their feet. With temperatures well below 20 degrees of frost the water froze immediately, and prisoners were left for hours with their feet frozen into the ice to "reflect" on their crimes.

'Many of the guards in charge of prisoners in solitary confinement were adept at this sort of brutality and seem to have been given full rein to stand prisoners to attention, spit on them, kick them, beat them, prod them with bayonets, wake them at odd times throughout the night and humiliate them at will. Such treatment was not exceptional; it was the normal fate of the prisoner who steadfastly refused to cooperate or who was sufficiently important to merit intensive "conditioning" . . .'

The truly horrifying thing about these accounts is the complete uselessness of the sufferings inflicted. Nothing was achieved and the value of the propaganda that could be extracted was nil. It is to be hoped that this has been amply demonstrated and the lesson learned, so that no-one will ever have recourse to such methods again.

THE AMERICAN DREAM AND THE POW

If Fate decrees that you are to spend some time as a POW, the best place in which to spend it has been the USA, where, even in World War I the standard of living and that provided for American troops and thus for POWs as well, was so high that to the ordinary European conscript it was like being translated to a different world. Once disembarked, the World War II prisoners of the US (there were more than 400 000 of them) were conveyed in upholstered railway coaches (in which they were served coffee and sandwiches) to their final destination. This was very likely a camp in the Southern States — a deliberate choice of location made to save on heating bills. Some of these camps were specially built for the POWs. They were spacious: lines of barracks built of pine timber, tarred paper and concrete, but fitted with adequate modern plumbing — a thing so often lacking and the cause of endless complaint from those in POW camps on the European Continent. Perhaps the only cause for complaint from the prisoner-occupants came from the climate, which was sometimes too hot for the average European. As this accommodation was the same as that provided by the US army for its own men, it was neither more nor less than what was required by the Geneva Convention.

The occupants were fortunate, indeed. Astounding, too, was the variety of goods to be bought in the canteens, greater and more luxurious than most of the POWs had enjoyed in civilian life. Rations were supplied to the same scale of cost as those given to the enlisted men (as laid down by the Geneva Convention), and the POWs were able to spend some of the money on providing their own specialities: various sausages, pig's trotters, etc. The prisoners cooked their own food and so prepared it in their own ways and to very high standards. Following European tradition, they turned scraps and bones into soups and stews, so that at least one contractor, who removed

A converted wine cask makes a convenient isolation cell when the real thing is not available. Constricted though the occupant is, these wine casks of the Spanish Civil War are spacious compared with the little boxes used by the North Koreans.

kitchen garbage, cancelled his contract because there was too little to make it worth his while.

Some of the German POWs refrained from mentioning the excellence of fare in their letters home, in case they might be accused of making American propaganda. Others did so, the refrain being that in these camps they ate more in a day than they had been accustomed to eat in a week. Another refrain was: no parcels, please — they are quite unnecessary.

In all camps there were the usual libraries, lectures on all sorts of subjects, and facilities for learning. There were amateur theatricals, concerts given by orchestras of POW musicians, with instruments supplied by the Red Cross and charitable institutions, gardens designed and maintained by the POWs (in Alabama even a topiary garden); the POWs played soccer, baseball and tennis; at Camp Crowder in Missouri they set up a zoo complete with aviary, the animals including alligators, white mice, monkeys and a pig. To occupy themselves, rather than from any need of extra cash, some POWs made souvenirs out of snakeskin which they sold to the guards, others painted still lifes, portraits, landscapes and battle-scenes from memory, and many of these were exhibited and sold. Apart from that one little factor, freedom, it could be said that they had never had it so good.

CHAPTER 6

WORK

The Geneva Convention of 1929 legalized the age-old usage that the prisoner of war must work for his keep. In antiquity, when all war was total, there was never question of anything else; your captive was yours to kill, sell or set to work. The state used the captives it did not sell for its most arduous tasks: mining, building, working the sweeps of naval and other ships, while the private purchaser might need a clerk, a gladiator, an agricultural labourer, anything. Sometimes, the main purpose of war in antiquity was to augment a country's labour force, as it was of many a Viking raid in the days of the expansion of northern agriculture before AD 1000. Many a purchaser of these slaves must have acquired human resources of much more value than just another pair of hands. One wonders too just how willing or unwilling those hands were? If the experience of the twentieth century is anything to go by, the true countryman has such a close, intimate relationship with the soil that he can never deny it its due. The history of this century's two world wars provides evidence of examples of POWs set to work in factories, who have deliberately spoiled material and produced things that would not work, but there are no stories of seed being deliberately destroyed, crops spoiled or harvests not brought in.

POWs have always been a valuable source of labour, from 480 BC when Gelon's victory over the Carthaginians at Himera provided Sicily with a huge work force, which was used on public works mainly in the cities, and especially in Agrigentum, to World War II, when POW labour had become essential for the economies of both Britain and the USA. Repatriation had to be adjusted so that labour was retained until demobilization of British and American troops had ensured the necessary replacements (as well as to allow the authorities to be certain that there were houses, food and jobs for the POWs to return to).

The POW was given the jobs nobody else wanted. The Athenians set the 20 000, mainly Persians, they captured at the Battle of the River Eurymedon to work in their silver mines at Laurion. Mining was a favourite job for POWs, for when Agesilaus, King of Sparta, captured Lampsacus, he freed a number of Greeks who proved to be former POWs who had escaped after being forced to work in the mines. The ancient Egyptians similarly worked numbers of their prisoners in their mines. POWs have been set to practically every job. Charlemagne's soldiers were often awarded one or more captives as part of their booty (and pay) and these became their serfs whom they could sell or send home to work for them there. The Church's edict of 1179 prohibiting the sale by Christians of fellow Christians as slaves was long disregarded — as late as the early eighteenth century, the Russians sold some of their Swedish prisoners to provincial landowners as serfs — but there came a time when there was no real shortage of labour and then prisoners who could not ransom themselves were often just stripped of what little they had and left to fend for themselves.

In the wars of the mid-seventeenth century, the numbers of prisoners taken seems to have been roughly equal on either side, so that the emphasis shifted to exchange. Prisoners were sent to safe places, far enough from home to deter them from trying to escape, and there they stayed until their exchange could be arranged. Later, in the wars between Russia and Sweden, when prisoners were distributed over vast areas and the Russian authorities seem to have had little or no idea of how many they had or where they were, it became accepted by either side that each was to feed, house and clothe its prisoners (officers excepted), who in return would work for their captors. Swedish POWs played a conspicuous part in designing and building Petersburg and other cities in Russia (such as Tobolsk) while the officers, dispersed far and wide thoughout the recently annexed lands of Siberia, explored and mapped the new lands, recording their flora and fauna and mineral wealth. It is thanks to them that Siberia was opened up.

In the Napoleonic Wars there seems to have been no need for POW labour, and prisoners only worked for themselves, in the sense that they made knick-knacks and ornaments to sell to the public and so provide a meagre supplement to their income. In the Crimea and the minor wars of the early part of this century, the numbers involved were not great enough to justify their use as labour, since the workforces of the belligerent nations were not affected.

In World War I, when both sides took large numbers of prisoners and armies were so huge that labour forces at home were often seriously depleted, it became necessary to turn again to POW labour. Most people prefer to be doing something rather than nothing. Before long, in Austria-Hungary, Germany, Tsarist Russia, Italy, France and Great Britain, POWs were at work building roads, in factories, on the railways, in forestry and above all on farms. Working outside the POW camps, prisoners came into direct contact with the civilian population. Soldiers, especially those who have actually fought, seldom hate each other, but propaganda which is aimed at improving the war effort, tends to promote hatred of the enemy among the civilian population. This caused occasional conflict with the Geneva Convention which requires the detaining power to protect prisoners from the abuse, jeers and ridicule of the civilian population. Such expressions of prejudice were usually very short-lived, especially if the prisoners concerned were willing workers.

This pattern was generally repeated in World War II, though here the differences between east and west in Europe were considerable. French, British, Dutch and US POWs in German hands were treated in accordance with international undertakings as far as local circumstances allowed; but the German prisoners in Russia and the Russian and other East European prisoners in German hands, were shamefully maltreated, partly because of ideological fantasies of racial inferiority and partly because their own standards were so different.

THE SIMPLE LIFE

Again, it was those who worked on farms who had the best of it. Elvet Williams has described in his *Arbeitskommando*, the place where he spent some months repairing the road up to a skiing resort not far from Linz in Austria. He and his companions were housed in a log cabin. There was no fence or barbed-wire round them. At night they were locked into their dormitory, latrine buckets having been provided, while their trousers were hung up on pegs in the passage outside with their boots neatly ranged underneath. Their surroundings he has described thus:

> 'The work site could not have been set in more idyllic surroundings; the wide, clear, chattering stream bounded merrily over its rocky bed in masses of spray; narrow waterfalls bounded down the hillside; wooded slopes rose endlessly to disappear into the bluest of skies; the valley wriggled and twisted to give a fresh view round every bend, and with every time of day and angle of sun. All round was a peace impossible to comprehend after the turmoil and carnage of Crete, enhanced rather than broken by the continuous sounds of rushing water and the incessant song of the birds. It might have been Shangri-la or Utopia . . .'

Equally fortunate were two Frenchmen in an agricultural Kommando, whose elderly guard's civilian profession, as far as he had one, had been that of poacher. The Kommando was working in good 'deer country' and the old poacher used to take the two Frenchmen with him when he went out to practice his civilian skills, and even let them have rifles so that they could hunt on their own. Unfortunately, one farmer over whose land they hunted felt that he was not getting his fair share of the venison and in his disgruntlement reported the poacher to the police. He was put away for ten years.

Similar sport was enjoyed by a German POW who worked on a 500-acre (200-hectare) farm somewhere in Britain. He was the only POW employed by the farmer who had no interest in shooting, while this particular POW was a keen shot, and so the farmer lent him his gun and let him go out in the early morning or evening to get a few rabbits or partridges for the pot.

The list of jobs that POWs in Germany and Britain were given to do is long and varied: working in a paper mill, taking hay to deer in the forest during a hard winter, demolition, clearing up after air raids, work in a pram factory, in a boot factory, unloading granite, unloading timber, laying drains, working in a brickyard, in forestry, as a tailor's assistant, in salt mines, in steel works and, above all, in agriculture. In Germany, however, Allied POWs were made to help produce munitions and in loading and transporting shells to the front in flagrant breach of the Geneva Convention. They were given jobs in mines considered too dangerous for German miners. They had to work in chemical factories where there was considerable risk of poisoning, and there were cases of POWs being made to help with AA guns during Allied air raids. In Britain POWs were not normally employed on military work of any kind. After the cessation of hostilities in World War II, German POWs in Britain and France were put to bomb

POWS at work in the fields. In World War II horses were still widely used in agriculture, thus saving precious petrol. Here the farmer or his steward is watching progress in the background, but there are no guards. The countryman, is at home anywhere in the fields and if he can get out of the camp and into them that is all he wants until peace is declared and he can get home.

disposal and mine-lifting on the grounds that each POW bore an individual, partial responsibility for the wickedness of his government, so that it was morally justifiable to exact that form of retribution.

Officers were not required to work (except those in Russian and Japanese hands), nor were senior NCOs. When really short of labour, the Germans did their best to trick, cajole or threaten NCOs into working. The French devised an ingenious method of circumventing these attempts. Francis Ambrière has described how this method was employed in March 1942 in a camp near Limburg, when 20 NCOs were sent under armed guard to unload coal for the Kommandatur.

'(They) fell in without a murmur, started off on the word of command and marched in disciplined fashion to their destination. There, when signs were made that they should take up tools, they, in the calmest manner in the world, said: "What! Are we supposed to work? Oh, then there's been some mistake. You must have picked the wrong hut. We're exempt from work under article 27 of the Geneva Convention."

Nothing disconcerted guards more than politeness, especially when it was accompanied by invoking the law, which always made them apprehensive in case they might in fact have gone too far and were heading for trouble. So, watched by the thunderstruck German railway workers, the Feldwebel in charge of this so-called work-party had to order an about turn and march the NCOs back to camp. There, the 20 were made to stand outside the Colonel's office for eight hours, but when the time came for the evening Appel, they were sent back to their huts, having won a victory for themselves and the whole camp.

TYPES OF KOMMANDO

Work for POWs in Germany was organized in Kommandos, of which there were four main types: a) those whose members normally worked on building and repairing roads or railway track (in these discipline was fairly rigorous); b) farming Kommandos in which work was hard (initially back-breaking for those not accustomed to it) but in its own way rewarding and often with its own perks (better or extra food and often some sex life); c) factory Kommandos in which POWs were expected to work hard and long, making all sorts of things to assist the war effort, and in these most POWs did their least and their utmost to botch, scrimp and sabotage.

A British POW employed in one of these factory Kommandos, E Ayling, has vividly described the attitudes of employer and employee:

> 'The Huns in general seemed absolutely unable to grasp the underlying reasons for our apparent inability to carry out efficiently our different tasks; and our lack of zeal, when they compared us with themselves. I don't think the passive resistance of the POW was ever really seen through. They just could *not* see why we did not rush to work, and classed one and all as lazy and stupid. Fortunately for us, perhaps, they did not seem to realize that in our minds they were at all times the *enemy*, and that, although without arms, "the war for you is *not* over" to adjust their standard phrase — we should attempt at least to do little things, if with milder methods, to slow up the Hitler machine just a little, and by so doing, help ourselves towards our cherished objective "Home as soon as possible". To annoy, to irritate, to bait.'

Lastly (d): there were town Kommandos for those in a variety of professions, each of whom worked at his own speciality and enjoyed almost complete freedom.

Neither the employers nor the guards who looked after the prisoners in these Kommandos were prepared for their role. When those in an agricultural Kommando reached the village, where they were to work, the poor POWs had to endure the equivalent of a slave market, as the peasant-farmers:

> 'circulated among the ranks of motionless prisoners, unhurriedly choosing their man for his size and muscles, while the late-comers protested with pointed fingers at the poor material that remained.'

Then came the realization that owing to ignorance (feigned or genuine) of the language, the employer had to show how he wanted the job done, rather than just tell them what he wanted. Many of the prisoners, especially those who had been peace-time conscripts in their armies and not sufficiently keen soldiers to apply in peace for officer status, were intellectually far superior to their employers, and as Francis Ambrière has described, in many cases the prisoners were soon teaching their employers:

> 'Thus between employers and employees there imperceptibly arose such an intermingling of functions that in a number of cases it was the Germans who slipped into the habit of taking orders from the French. Gradually this habit spread from the work to other aspects of existence. After twelve months or more of captivity, spent beneath the roof of some peasant or small contractor, it was not unusual at meal times to see

Russian prisoners of the Austrians working as lumberjacks during World War I. Here again there are no guards in sight.

Turkish prisoners of the British in World War I being put to work building a road under the all-seeing eye of a British NCO. The local spades and picks have unusually long handles. With a workforce of this size things get done quickly — as the Pharaohs knew.

the aged head of the family seeking the advice of his prisoner on the most diverse matters; while the latter, according to his character, would give a lofty or sympathetic answer, mingling with the Platt-deutsch that he had willy-nilly acquired, a few sonorous French oaths which freed him of any feeling of humiliation.

'Although this was a fact of major psychological interest, it generally went unnoticed, because one had to be a very close observer of all the phenomena of captivity to perceive its existence at all. Nevertheless, it explains a great many things; not least, the fact that a number of prisoners, agreeably flattered by an audience which they had not had at home, preferred to stay on in some small town of Hesse or Saxony, rather than return to their own country . . .'

No one, to quote Francis Ambrière, 'in our state of general deprivation could endure captivity without instinctively clinging to some value which corresponded to his innermost nature'. The mystics had their God, or they rediscovered him; the reflective, the introverts, could have recourse to the inner life of meditation, while the dreamers could live in books; but the most fortunate were the peasants with their inalienable love of the soil. Their fellow prisoners, from the towns and cities would laugh at them when they referred in their talk to *their* oxen, *their* cows, *their* plough, but this was inevitable. The worker on the land cannot help identifying himself with

whatever he is cultivating. These peasants in the Kommandos rediscovered in that other country the familiar rhythms of their life at home, and the passage of the seasons was no different when observed beneath a foreign sky. They were what they had always been: wholly obedient to the pulse of Nature and absorbed in the unremitting labours of the land. In many instances they took over imperceptibly, but completely. In many of the villages where they worked all the men had been conscripted into the army and the Kommando peasants were dealing only with the old, the women and children; thus on them devolved the whole authority and prestige of the male. There was no competition; thus, just as they had had to replace the absent head of the family in the fields, it was almost inevitable that they should replace him in the family bed as well, as if the farmer's wife went with the farm.

On the whole, the POW employed in agriculture in Germany, Great Britain or wherever during World War II was a relatively happy man. A British agricultural engineer who employed a number of Germans mainly on putting derelict farms back into production, comparing them with the German POWs of World War I (of whom he had also had experience) was struck by the defiant attitude of some of the World War II POWs, a sort of 'we may be prisoners, but we're not beaten yet,' whereas their fathers in World War I had been what he called 'sportsmen'. However, both lots were good workers. They started at eight or nine o'clock and left off at dusk.

Sometimes they were working two or three miles out in the country without guards and could easily have set on him, but he never had any trouble. Whatever time of day he paid them a visit, he said, he always found them working. According to him, what you got out of the POW depended on how you treated him, but it must in part have depended on the kind of work you asked him to do.

As a rule the German POW working on the land achieved an excellent relationship with his employer. One in France wrote:

> 'In December we were distributed among the farmers in the village. I was sent to the Burgermeister's, where I was well off. I ate with the family, eating and drinking whatever I liked. My boss bought me trousers, a shirt and shoes, so that I became human again. I had to work in the fields and in the vineyard. My boss treated me as his own son. He had himself been a prisoner in Germany until 1944, and he told me that as he had been treated by his farmer in Württemberg, so would he treat me.'

Another account, this one of life in Britain:

> 'There were three of us on the farm, and it was rather nice. Eight hours work. We catered for ourselves, and on the whole we were well pleased to have done with camp life . . . After he had got over his initial mistrust, the farmer was perfectly friendly and pleased with us. We often worked on our own . . . In February the farmer asked for me back. I was alone. I ate at the farmer's table and had nothing to complain of . . .'

In many ways the great thing was to be away from the ghastly camp:

> 'Franz and I have now become gardeners: speciality — tomatoes and chrysanthemums. We are set down at a certain place and off we go to work whistling merrily. Our lady employer has two delightful poodles which greet us with joyful barks. They are allowed that, as the fraternization ban does not apply to dogs. We often work with two of the women, who quite simply see past us. The foreman who gives us our jobs hardly speaks to us otherwise, but the work is fun.'

By the Spring of 1946 conditions in France were such that:

> '. . . we could visit each other every Sunday. We were lent bicycles to go to the farthest place. We were able to go anywhere in a 10 km radius without being abused by civilians or having any difficulties from the police. Our (woman) boss had even got it agreed that our clothes need not be daubed with the usual PG, for normally even our underclothes were thus decorated. . . . (My pal and I) had the same ration cards for food as the civilians; at meals nothing was kept from us; in fact we ranked at table immediately after the *patron* and the first hand, and after us all the others including madame, even when there were visitors. We were thoroughly absorbed into the great family. In the two other places in the village, the others were just as well off. We were allowed to listen to the radio, no doors were locked to us and on many Sundays we were left to ourselves.'

Harder than work on the land and without the latter's advantages of being healthy and satisfying was the traditional labour of the captive: mining. One German POW has described how in Thiers-la-Grange in northern France, after a superficial medical examination had pronounced them fit to work in the mines, they were given new work-clothes and allocated to three different shifts and put to work:

> 'I had never seen a mine from outside, let alone inside. For 95% of us POWs the work was completely unfamiliar. There were many accidents and deaths, because we were not aware of the dangers. Without basic training or instruction, which in ordinary life a miner recruit would obviously be given, such results were inevitable. We were hustled at work. Who didn't complete his stint, had to go down another time. Again the French were still working seams that to us seemed thoroughly uneconomic. . . .'

Another German POW-miner writing about Faulquemont near Saint-Avold (Moselle) has described how:

> 'At the end of the shift we again had to wait until all the others had left. A true medley of peoples crowded round the door of the cage: Poles, Russians, Ukrainians, Maroccans, etc. If one of us cheated and was discovered, there were always blows. Going down about 6 o'clock, we were back in the day-light about 2 o'clock in the afternoon.
>
> 'We soon noticed that not much attention was paid to safety or accident-prevention. There was no time for that. Coal was more important.'

If a British POW was injured or killed at work, it was regarded as being on active service and he or his dependents were entitled to the same pension or compensation as those killed or injured in battle, but there was no such provision for German POWs, who were thus at a considerable disadvantage. (No German POW was employed in a British mine.)

There are hundreds of books describing the lot of the prisoners of the Japanese in World War II. Men and officers alike were treated as slaves, made to work on the most arduous tasks for the maximum time on the minimum of food, without hygiene or medical attention. History provides no examples of graver maltreatment of human beings, and that this could happen in the twentieth century will remain one of the puzzles of the history of man. Yet here again, as so often, some were less badly off than others. For some to be sent on an up-country work party was indeed a dreadful thing:

> 'for it means extremely unpleasant and tiring journeys, short rations and as a rule very hard work. Also one is more under the direct authority of the Nips. One is more in touch with disease, malaria, dysentery etc. and often drugs are short, especially if the party is away for over a month or six weeks. The parties always come back in a very bad state of health and, more than likely, minus a few of the party who have died. This time — I think I have said this before — I have come out of hospital fitter than I've been since we came to Thailand and feel capable of harder work. I don't feel the strain as I used to. It's grand to feel like this — TOUCH WOOD — let's hope this state continues . . .'

For others being sent upcountry on a work party was a death sentence.

In the early part of World War II the Allies took few prisoners, though the Dutch managed to capture some and ship them to Britain before they themselves were overwhelmed and these gave them a slight lever when bargaining with their enemy. The few prisoners taken by the British were sent mostly to Canada to be out of the way. Captured when Germany's fortunes were in the ascendant, they were convinced of their country's ultimate victory and their arrogant, recalcitrant attitude made them useless as a workforce and work was not made mandatory until August 1944, when help was needed with the grain harvest.

In Korea, the UN forces had no possibility of putting their prisoners to work. It was all the authorities could do to contain them within their camps, and this led to the 57th report of the UN Command (November 1–5, 1952) stating that a Communist was to be regarded:

> 'Not as a passive being in need of care and protection until he could be returned to his home, but as still an active soldier determined to fight on in whatever way his leader dictated.'

The Italians captured in North Africa were sent to Australia, India, South Africa as well as to Britain where the 3000 POWs working there in 1941 had grown to 75 000 at the end of 1943, mainly employed in agriculture. Of these latter some 7000 were billeted on farmers, who needed only a few each, the others worked from camps of some 500 going out daily in groups of a dozen or more to farms within a 25-mile radius. Others were employed on drainage and reclamation schemes, in forestry, mining, road-repair and, as always, loading and unloading railway waggons. When Italy entered the war on the Allies' side and thus became a 'cobelligerent', Italian POWs could legitimately be employed making munitions of war.

Apart from the Germans and Italians captured in North Africa, the great majority of Axis prisoners were taken when the Allies realized that they were indeed going to win the war and the Axis that it had to all intents and purposes already lost. The attitude of the captor/victor to his prisoners tended to be more lenient and not vindictive, while the POW was all too aware that there was no point in trying to escape and continue the struggle, as that would inevitably soon be over. POW workers saw that sabotaging or hampering production was consequently useless. Most POWs were glad to be able to work, firstly because it gave them something to do. They were able to talk to their employers and even to make friends with them, and they could earn money. *Prisoners of England* quotes a German, son of a Hamburg carpenter, who was brought to England early in 1945, started work at Harwell helping to lay foundations for prefabs, then did some work on a farm:

> 'There the people were extremely nice. I was the only POW there and I always got biscuits and a can of coffee with lots of milk. I sat in the barn by myself drinking it. I did enjoy it. We were all taken to work by an army truck and dropped off at various places. There was no hate relationship, even with the guards. We got on quite well with them. We were also used on building roads . . . I drove a dumper shifting earth. We helped build roads and sewer systems. What firms did, which they were not supposed to do, was to give us a couple of pounds, which provided incentive to work harder. There was a little shop I used to go to with a fellow POW who spoke English and buy cotton, safety pins and needles to send home, because these things were in short supply there. The shopkeepers were very good to us, though you'd get one or two who were less friendly. We wore army uniforms with patches (green, yellow, red) so that we were distinguishable (otherwise they were standard British army uniforms). There were holes cut under the patches so that we couldn't take the patches off. However, friends had given us old raincoats, so we slipped them over our uniforms when we

went into a shop (the friends were people who worked on the building site). We always supplemented our food . . .'

FROM PRISON CAMP TO TOY FACTORY

Other ways of earning money were the traditional ones of the prisoner, at least since the Napoleonic Wars, of making things to sell out of things found, stolen, or bought. Alf Eiserback writing of Didcot Camp in Berkshire records:

'The camp itself at night was like a workshop. Everyone worked like mad, making toys. It was like a factory. They were then sold for cigarettes. The most impossible things were made there: dachshunds on wheels, with rubber in the middle so that when they were pulled along they wiggled; chickens on a wooden board who pecked when elastic was pulled. We also made suitcases out of plywood. We took tools from the depot. One tent even had a complete dentist's outfit, which it used for engraving. Unfortunately this was missed and had to be returned. I didn't do much. I did the selling and got commission. As I was driving, it was easy to get the stuff out of the camp. Even the police at the gate bought toys from us. After that, they couldn't stop us any more. We had free run of the depot and could take anything we wanted.'

The US sent all its prisoners back to the States, if only because that saved them using men of the expeditionary forces to guard them (though one American writer has asserted that towards the end of the war the Americans found it possible anywhere in the Communization Zone to work groups of hundreds of German POWs without any guards whatsoever and, as a result, in 1944 the US Army was able to disband most of the Military Police companies assigned to guarding POWs in the Zone of the Interior). It was also less costly to use the food and clothes needed at the source of production rather than ship it all abroad. This fact opened the eyes of 124 000 Germans and 50 000 Italians to the high standard of living in the USA. The USA scrupulously followed the regulations of the Geneva Convention and provided its POWs with accommodation and rations equal to those provided for its own troops; that this was luxury, if not undreamed-of riches to very many of them, made no difference.

In Europe, once hostilities had ceased in World War II, there was little point in continuing to guard POWs. They might require supervision to ensure that they earned their keep, but as they were bound to be repatriated in accordance with the Geneva Convention, as soon as conditions in their ravaged country allowed, and there was so obviously no point in trying to jump the gun, experiments were made in a number of camps, (notably Featherstone Park Camp in Northumberland) whereby German officers who volunteered for work and signed the requisite undertaking were allowed to work on farms or drainage schemes without guards. No one took advantage of the opportunity to break their undertaking.

In the last two World Wars, in Europe and America, POW labour has been a godsend; indeed, none of the combatants could have lasted out so long without it. Agricultural work on farms in particular has been important to the POWs, providing real therapy for the ills of captivity and often leading to friendship and even marriage. The sense of shared purpose and the achievement of work well done together was epitomized by the scene at a parish church in Hexham, Northumberland, on a Sunday in November 1946. The church was filled with a thousand German POWs and 300 Northumberland farmers come to join in thanking their God for a good harvest safely garnered.

A pencil drawing by F Staeger of Russian POWs of the Austrians breaking stone for roadmaking during World War I.

A painting by Albert Janesch of Serbians captured by Austrians in World War I.

Art behind wire — creativity and the POW

Several of the illustrations in this book are drawings or paintings by artists who have been POWs. Once an army absorbs more than just the professional soldier every sort of civilian occupation will be found among the prisoners in the camp. This will include artists, actors, theatrical producers, musicians, conductors, variety artists, etc. Talent let alone genius is not stifled by imprisonment, though the artist's thoughts are likely to be turned inwards upon his own predicament. His main difficulty has always been to obtain suitable materials. Much of what artists have drawn or painted must have been lost; but the pictures reproduced here provide a sample of what they have done.

36. Défense de sortir des ba-
raques après 6 heures
(comment ils observaient
les consignes)

Stern interpretation of the
curfew law in one camp; a
cartoon by Jean Morin.

CHAPTER 7

THE EFFECTS OF CAPTIVITY

The personification of defeat and surrender. Utter dejection on the face of a German POW — the face of one for whom perhaps capture is the end of this world.

The gates of a POW camp may clang shut behind the new arrival with something of the same resonance as the door of the civil prison cell, but the state of mind of the two 'new boys' is somewhat different. The civilian prisoner knows that he has done something for which society is making him atone, and he knows the length of the process of atonement, whereas the POW (other than the captured Japanese soldier for whom surrender or capture are equally shameful, and the Soviet warrior to whom they were forbidden) has no sense of guilt or of justice being done to him, nor has he any idea of the length of his imprisonment, for no sentence has been passed.

To quote from the diary of Major E Booth:

'One of the merciful dispensations at the commencement of captivity was that a state of physical exhaustion prevented one from suffering greatly from the pangs of imprisonment and from the knowledge of separation for an indefinite period from home and family. At first, food and rest were all that could be thought of; later, when we were rested and recovered, everyone had to make up his mind in his own way to being a prisoner.'

The prisoner's immediate need is usually rest, but once rested, there is an emotional adjustment to be made. Yesterday he was free and fighting the enemy, today he is in the enemy's hands and Geneva Convention or no Geneva Convention, at his mercy, especially in the Far East where attitudes to war and the value of human life are so different. In World War II, the Japanese told their captives that they were not deemed prisoners of war at all, but merely slave labour, to be used at will and disposed of when no longer required. This is a shocking attitude to those brought up on the

Geneva Convention, but it has a long history, for it was that of Alexander the
Great, the ancient Egyptians and Charlemagne, as well as of the Germans
towards their Slavonic prisoners and of the Russians towards *all* their
prisoners in World War II.

The first proper accounts of how confinement affects the prisoner of
war come from the French, Dutch and Americans imprisoned in the so-
called depôts of Norman Cross and Dartmoor during the Napoleonic Wars.
The French prisoners in Dartmoor divided themselves into five categories:
Les Lords, who were men of good family in receipt of funds from home and
thus not in any need, especially if they accepted parole and lived outside a
camp; then there were *Les Laboureurs*, men who buckled to and made knick-
knacks and things to sell locally and used the money thus earned to supplement their rations; there were, too, *Les Indifferents*, the apathetic, who did
nothing but lounge about, making do with what rations they were given;
then *Les Miserables* who were the gamblers and hatchers of mischief; but the
really extraordinary phenomenon is the extremes to which gambling was
carried by *Les Romains* (Romans). In their behaviour there may have been
an element of revolt against the trammels of social law. As one commentator
wrote:

> 'The evolution of the Romans was natural enough. The gambling fever
> seized upon the entire prison, and the losers, having nothing but their
> clothes and bedding to stake, turned these into money and lost them.
> Unable to obtain other garments, and feeling themselves shunned by
> their former companions, they betook themselves to the society of men
> as unfortunate as themselves, and went to live in the cockloft, because
> no one who lived in the more desirable floors cared to have them as
> neighbours. As they grew in numbers they began to feel a pride in their
> isolation, and to persuade themselves that they had come to it by their
> own choice. In imitation of the floors below, where a "Commissaire"
> was chosen by public election, and implicitly obeyed, they elected some
> genial, devil-may-care rascal to be their "General", who only held office
> because he never attempted to enforce his authority in the interests of
> decency and order. At the end of the first six months the number of
> admitted Romans was 250, and in the later years it exceeded 500,
> although the number was always fluctuating. In order to qualify for the
> Order it was necessary to consent to the sale of every remaining garment
> and article of bedding for the purchase of tobacco for the use of the
> community. The communism was complete. Among the whole 500
> there was no kind of private property, except a few filthy rags, donned
> as a concession to social prejudice . . . A few old blankets held in
> common, with a hole in the middle for the head like a poncho, were used
> by those whose business took them into the yards.
>
> 'In the Capitole itself everyone lived in a state of nudity, and slept
> naked on the concrete floor, for the only hammock allowed was that of
> the "General", who slept in the middle and allocated the lairs of his
> constituents. To this end a rough sort of discipline was maintained, for
> whereas 500 men could sleep without much discomfort on a single floor
> in three tiers of hammocks, the actual floor space was insufficient for
> more than a third of that number of human bodies lying side by side.
> At night, therefore, the Capitole must have been an extraordinary
> spectacle. The floor was carpeted with nude bodies, all lying on the
> same side, . . . it was impossible to get a foot between them.

'At nightfall, the "General" shouted "Fall in", and the men ranged themselves in two lines facing one another. At a second word of command, alternate files took two paces to the front and rear and closed inward, and at the word *"Bas"*. they all lay down on their right sides. At intervals during the night the "General" would cry *"Pare à viser* (Attention), "A Dieu, Va!" and they would all turn over.'

There could hardly be a better example of the power of gambling fever than the fact that these men would pledge all or part of their daily rations to the camp's entrepreneur food merchants to get money or tobacco with which to gamble. Some of the Romans were men of good family and in receipt of a regular remittance from home, usually paid quarterly. When the money arrived, the recipient would borrow a suit of clothes in which to go to the Agent's Office to collect it. He would then hand over £1 to the General, which was spent on tobacco or food for the community, kit himself out with clothes and bedding and resume life as a normal being on one of the floors for as long as his money lasted. When he had lost it all, he sold the clothes and bedding, as before, lost that money and returned to the cockloft, where he would be given a boisterous welcome.

Decent prisoners always made tremendous efforts to help these poor devils from going Roman again, but they never could. And yet, although one would have thought that when the gambling urge was so strong, these people would have ended up in the gutters of their home towns after their release and some may well have done just that, not by any means all did. There are authenticated cases of one taking holy orders and becoming a village priest, another became a high government official, while others turned into successful business men.

In 1813, 14 Romans entitled to an issue of new clothing were caught, scrubbed from top to toe, properly clothed and so returned to their fellows; but by the next day they had sold every stitch and were stark naked again.

These men would never have degenerated into this state but for the existence of fellow prisoners prepared to buy their rations from them for resale to other prisoners. These exploiters, as we would call them today, have been found in all POW camps ever since, even in the Japanese camps of World War II, and probably they have always existed. As the 'Bamboo Doctor' remarked, in those extreme conditions, very few of the POWs seemed to have retained any sense of decency or responsibility and little or no interest in the principle of fair shares. Stanley Pavillard was the so-called Bamboo Doctor, in origin a Spaniard who, having trained as a doctor in Edinburgh, took a job as medical officer to bank employees in Singapore. When they, as members of the Volunteer Defence Force, were marched off into captivity, he voluntarily went with them, suffering with them and treating them as best he could. He was witness to the fact that people lived by their cunning and wits, sometimes pulling their rank to achieve an unfair advantage. The weak went to the wall.

In his account of his own captivity in Europe in World War II, Stuart Brown castigates himself and his fellows as 'a greedy grasping bunch of egocentrics, each and everyone with few exceptions terrified lest the other "won" that little extra.' It was a free-for-all society in which normal courtesies were discarded through selfishness.

For quite a number the struggle to survive was just too much effort and they gave up. These were the 'wire-happy', identifiable by 'a glazed look, apologetic grin and clothes untidier than most.'

In a way this is akin to the cynical view of some conscripts nurtured on the old saying of World War I that war was 90 per cent waiting and ten per cent frenzied activity. This view was that, except for the professional soldier, war by its very nature is bound to be a complete waste of time, and those of that cynical turn of mind were sometimes inclined to think that they might as well waste their time in Germany as anywhere else. Those who can think in those terms, of course, are getting enough to eat and can have no idea of the effects of extreme physical deprivation.

THE LIFE-GIVING RED CROSS PARCEL

The unfortunate men who endured the extreme conditions of POW camps in the Far East or in Russia are the ones who know what real hunger and thirst can do to a man. The accounts of their captivity provided by Germans returned from POW camps in Russia emphasize again and again how hunger 'as our primal, strongest driving force unmasks man in the most gruesome way, reveals the frailty of the social manners of our traditional upbringing'. It came as a shock to many to discover what people were like once the mask of social convention had been removed:

'One's thoughts revolve almost exclusively round food. It is difficult not to be swept away by this undertow that reduces man to beast, and to retain one's dignity as a man even in the direst distress, in the continual torment of hunger.'

'Nobody knows how tremendously difficult it makes it, when this gnawing, boring, thrusting, demanding sensation from the pit of one's stomach paralyzes one's will and understanding, when wasting away leaves a gaping void in one's brain. In such conditions people become either brutes who disregard every rule of society and just fight for naked self-preservation, or they become silently long-suffering people, who, in their own minds, have finished with everything and are merely waiting for the end.'

The degrees of hunger experienced by POWs in Eastern Europe were not known in the West, except perhaps on rare occasions when in transit. For this POWs have largely to thank the Red Cross parcel which saved so many lives and minds. They were, however, common in Japanese camps in the Philippines, Malaya, Burma, etc.

Junior NCOs and ORs have always been expected to work while in captivity, an arrangement confirmed by the international conventions (though the stipulation that the work should not be of military benefit to the captor is under modern conditions impossible to fulfil). They have been put to work in agriculture, on road-building, in forests, factories, paper-mills, and in many other ways, and this has largely proved an agreeable way to pass the time, keep fit and, usually, improve diet. In these latter respects it is perhaps unfortunate that the international conventions have stipulated that officers and senior NCOs should not be required to perform manual work, so that they have had to rely solely on their own mental resources.

Elvet Williams was one who worked, mostly on repairing and extending a mountain road to a ski-resort an hour or so by rail from Linz. Of this he wrote:

'. . . the work itself would not have been the worst means of getting through the monotony of captivity. Most of it took place outside the barbed-wire. It began to toughen men up again, although most would have opted for getting fattened up first. The most salutary effect was on the brooders. They could not remain completely unresponsive to work: it got them off their bunks, however unwillingly, and thrust them, not too brutally, into company not of their own choosing; it loosened their

Food — the POW's perpetual obsession

Food has always been the main preoccupation of the POW, especially of the officers in World War I and II who had no work to occupy them. The rations provided, supposed to be the same as for the army of the detaining power, were often inadequate — sometimes intentionally, sometimes unintentionally — but in Europe (except Russia) they could be eked out with Red Cross parcels and canteen food. Food was cooked by the POWs themselves in messes of any number from one up. These drawings from Gordon Horner's *For You The War Is Over* are an amusing record of the POW's daily round.

Separating weevils from rice

The share-out

Gavi hunger spin

Condensato—five shillings a tin, but worth it

The scavenger

muscles and tongues, and, in spite of themselves, it forced them to swear, sometimes even to laugh. Even for the rest of us, work had a similar beneficial effect, admitted by no one at the time, causing us to rub shoulders and exchange talk with others not normally of our company . . .'

A German POW who worked in France, wrote this about it:

'Hard and unremitting as the community work was, it was healthy. We enjoyed the natural surroundings, were always in the open air, worked without shirts on and hardened ourselves. At first, having been ill, I found the work very hard, and often I thought that I would not be able to turn up again the next day, yet the next morning there I was again. Rather like an ageing car battery that is quickly charged and as quickly runs down again. Now, after almost a month's work I have improved physically and morally quite considerably, for, I again think of other things than just food.'

WORK PRESERVES SANITY

Work must have saved the lives and sanity of many. It calls for considerable strength of character and intellect to be confined and inactive. George Putnam, who was a prisoner in Virginia during 1864-5, has described how during the first two years of the war, there was little difference in class or, for that matter, intelligence between ORs and officers; but as the war progressed the ineffective officers were weeded out and replaced by men promoted from the ranks and made officers because they had shown that they had capacity. It became apparent that, on the whole, these were men of better education and greater intelligence — and they had more will-power. 'It was this will-power, this decision to live if possible, the unwillingness to give up, be beaten by the Confederacy or by circumstances, that helped during the last winter of war to save the lives of a number of starving officers.'

George Putnam is instructive on the question of the need to have something to do:

'The desire of occupation, whether in the way of amusement or instruction, was not merely for the purpose of passing the time. We realized in looking about the room that unless our minds or at least our thoughts, could be kept busy in some fashion, there was a risk of stagnation that might easily develop into idiocy. I recall a number of cases in which men who, as their vitality diminished, had lost the power of hopefulness, had lost also the control of their wills; their faces became vacant and in the more serious cases their conscious intelligence disappeared. These men would sit twisting their thumbs or would stand looking out of the windows with a vacant stare and with eyes that saw nothing.'

The importance of having an occupation, something to do, is well illustrated by the effect of giving the American prisoners in Dartmoor during the Napoleonic Wars, an extra allowance of one-and-a-half pence a day to enable them to purchase tobacco and soap. The money for this came from America. Basil Thomson has described the effect of this:

'It is very curious to see that this not too princely income of 1½d a day changed the whole mental attitude of the prisoners at a flash, and substituted order for anarchy. This little prison community was the great world in miniature, where, when men possess no private property, nor means of acquiring it, there is no play for the qualities of thrift, industry or honesty, but give them the power of acquiring private property, however small, and straightaway enterprise and the instinct of social order, spring up like grass after an April shower. We shall see further how, when a body of grown men are started fair with an equal income, even without the spur of having a family to provide for, in a matter of a few weeks the money has passed from the lazy and improvident into the hands of the industrious and the thrifty. When the love of acquisition ceases to be rooted in the fibre of human nature, the dream of socialists may be realized.'

THE DANGERS OF INACTIVITY

The realization that inactivity could lead to idiocy has led all officer POWs since the days of the French prisoners in Norman Corss and other English camps during the Napoleonic Wars, (and probably much earlier) to organize lectures and study-groups. John Mansell in his diaries of his captivity in World War I mentions lectures on Rhodesia and all sorts of other subjects; he mentions an Arts & Crafts Exhibition, theatricals and people playing chess, bezique, roulette, crown and anchor, etc.

In World War II it was the same story, as Major E Booth records:

'. . . in the early days at Laufen we filled most of our days by attending lectures on the most improbable subjects, poultry-farming, wine, the Bible, bee-keeping, and all evening we played bridge; at Warburg ninety per cent of the camp were engaged in toasting (escape) activities, while at Eichstatt examinations and sport held alternate sway as the seasons changed. All, to some extent, are forms of escapism, a desperate attempt to create at least the appearance of useful occupation. And yet, the POW even though he has no duties, work or responsibilities, has the feeling of living in a continual hurry, a continual fear that he may be missing something, a cup of tea, a bit of wood for the fire, another helping of soup, a good book. He feels an irresistible temptation to join the tail of any queue he may see without knowing what may be the object, for all good things in kriegie life are obtained either by waiting interminably or by working a racket . . .

'I am afraid all of us have become petty-minded to a greater or lesser extent: the most trivial deviation in the regular routine of our daily life takes on a formidable proportion. Moving quarters from Block I to Block III is a far more weighty undertaking than was any trip abroad; while getting the division on the move was child's play compared with moving a few hundred POWs from camp to camp . . .'

'Most POWs erect some sort of defence against the habits of their fellows and the majority, fortunately, recognize that every man has some habits distasteful to his neighbour, determining to ignore what they themselves don't like — usually with success . . .'

People accustomed to privacy suffered from the overcrowding that occurred in practically all camps and from lack of space. To quote Major E Booth:

'. . . the frustration is something which no one who has not been a prisoner-of-war will be able to understand, for in this crowded life, even now when our needs by early comparison are so well supplied, there is not enough of anything to go round; above all there is not enough space, and as for privacy that is non-existent . . . I don't suppose, either, that it is easy to understand how tired one gets of living with the same people for prolonged periods when "living", includes washing, dressing, shaving in close proximity.'

Turkish POWs in a Russian camp playing a sort of bowls during World War I.

The same was felt by the Germans in British camps. A booklet describing the situation of Camp 18 (Featherstone Park in Bedfordshire) in the summer of 1945, records:

'About 80 men lodged in each hut: apart from the beds, the only furniture consisted of two tables and four benches. Prisoners squatted on the edge of the bed, or lay on the two-tiered bunks. There was not a single moment of real peace to be obtained anywhere because one was continuously surrounded by games of cards, stories, discussions, lessons and other noises. There was also the summer heat. . . . always the same faces, the same voices, the same conversation, the same environment. . . .'

Among those who found captivity most irksome in the early days of World War I, before the Red Cross had been able to organize proper distribution of its parcels, were the smokers. To quote John Mansell again:

'July 13 . . . no cigarettes yet. With an occasional smoke one doesn't mind a number of little things that are irritating — presumably it has the effect of keeping one's nerves quiet. But with nothing to smoke, these same things tend to become unbearable, and people get on one's nerves — poor devils for the most harmless offences . . .'

Hans Reckel, a German POW of World War II, has recalled how smokers were especially prone to depression when unable to get tobacco. They found the enforced abstinence from nicotine 'extraordinarily painful. . . . The most addicted had long since sold their wedding rings to English soldiers — that is to say, swapped them for cigarettes'.

These pictures of the withdrawal symptoms suffered by those abruptly deprived of tobacco recall the so-called crusade of Amédée VI, in which the

French were soundly beaten at Nicopolis (September 25, 1396) and the accounts of how the French prisoners in the hands of the Turks, mostly young nobles, suffered by being deprived of the wine that had been the sole drink of most of them since infancy.

The body may be infinitely adaptable, but the process is sometimes slow and painful — and hard on the nerves. As John Mansell wrote:

SOLITARY CONFINEMENT IS A BLESSING

'March 13 . . . Living as we have been, and particularly as we are now, nerves are bound to be strained and it only requires the slightest spark to set things going. My own policy is to agree with anything. The moment I feel at all enraged with anyone, I try immediately to put myself in the other fellow's place and in 9 cases out of 10 his argument is perfectly sound and annoyance at it at once appears stupid.

But it is not only arguments. Habits are far worse, and the more insignificant and harmless they are, the more they drive one crazy. I'm not suggesting that I haven't got such habits myself — I know some that in others I would find equally infuriating. Everyone has his particular habits which in normal circumstances one would never think of taking offence at. I will illustrate a few in our room: the fellow who always hums to himself very quietly when he is reading or you are talking to him. The man who persistently strokes the long ends of his moustache with his tongue. The man who quietly spits out stray ends of tobacco from his cigarette, who eats abnormally slowly and endlessly chews a bit of nothing which I myself have swallowed in one. The man who dresses slowly and meticulously, looking no better for it, if anything rather a twirp . . .'

In effect, privacy could only be achieved in the punishment cells, provided that they too were not crowded. This is well expressed in Major E Booth's diary:

'March 31. I am writing this entry in my diary in one of the cells, for I have got myself a sentence of seven days close confinement with my hands tied behind my back for twelve hours a day, this because I was discovered by a Feldwebel without handcuffs (a punishment imposed in retaliation for alleged ill-treatment of German officer POWs in Canada, where they had briefly to sleep on the ground because they had deliberately burned their own beds.) It is a commuting sort of life that I lead now, because at nine pm I return to the camp to sleep and am fetched back here by the guard at eight o'clock next morning. The tying of hands behind the back is a farce, this much will appear from the writing of this diary; on the credit side is the wonderful sense of privacy and quiet, all the more welcome in that I am not completely cut off — meals are taken al fresco in the passage way in company with other inmates, and moreover at night I return to the outer world and hear all about the current day's events. On the debit side is the loss of exercise. We get out for an hour a day only . . . then I miss my usual occupations, particularly the gramophone and playing the recorder with Jimmy Dizer and his fiddle (what an excellent combination violin and recorder make, by the way) and I suppose it is inevitable that, at times, the hours should seem to pass slowly. Sometimes, when I am depressed, I feel that I have lost the art of being still in the constant hubbub of the last three years; it is not that I haven't done any silent thinking — only too often my mind goes racing away on some meteoric flight — but that even my thinking,

Religion was a comfort to those who had faith, but it is remarkable how few POWs, who were not practicing members of a congregation, found religion in a camp or even reverted to their childhood's convictions. These latter were probably an unquestioning acceptance of what they were told they should believe, without understanding or conviction. There is seldom real faith before adulthood.

when walking alone or when lying wakefully on my bed, has been in a way a frenzied reaction from the pettiness of prison life. Sometimes I feel that I have been so completely engulfed in this pettiness that the most important factor in my life has been reduced to the next meal or an extra cup of tea and that gradually my power of affection has withered, leaving nothing but an egotistically centred shell. Perhaps all of this is conjured up because now, for the first time in nearly three years, for a week on end I spend practically the whole of every day in a 'room' to myself; I can read without continual interruptions, without constantly being jostled in my chair, without being reminded that it is time to do this or that, to collect a parcel or fetch the soup. I can indulge my thoughts without having those of others thrust upon me.'

Crowding, particularly overcrowding, has a disastrous effect, especially when there is no prospect of an end to it in the foreseeable future. To quote one who returned from the ghastly camps for German POWs in Russia:

'Living together in such close proximity, in so little space, month after month and year after year; one got to know each other to the tiniest detail; each stood before the other, naked, bared, stripped of all social polish, showing himself as he really was. That was often terrifying.'

The shock of seeing people as they were was particularly great for those accustomed to look up to those higher in the social scale than themselves. They had been taught to expect too much:

'First shock: the collapse of the order in which one had previously believed and thought to be soundly constructed. Men, to whom one had previously looked up, suddenly revealed themselves as merely human, people for whom the "I" was more important than the ideals of sticking together, obedience and comradeship that they had used to emphasize. Gone was the iron discipline of esprit de corps. Instead, each became more and more suspicious of everyone else.'

John Mansell was captured in the very early days of World War I and spent four years in captivity. Young and inexperienced, he was plagued by doubts as to whether he had done the right thing in surrendering, whether he might not have acted differently. As the years passed and others taken prisoner much later came to the camps, John Mansell was almost tormented by the thought of what 'his war' had been:

'Talks with some of the newcomers rub in more than ever how much we have missed during the last $3\frac{1}{2}$ years. What in God's name will *we* have to talk about after the war — absolutely nothing, but sitting on one's backside in a POW camp, complaining of this and that which were in actual fact probably a great deal better than the conditions of those who are doing our work for us. The more I think about it, the more depressed I get and that is the chief reason why I can't bear listening to the stories of the new arrivals.'

'BARBED-WIRE HAPPINESS'

The state of mind of the POW, of course, is as varied as the men themselves. Elvet Williams has described how at times a sense of absolute freedom would come over him. This sense, he felt, could never have been experienced anywhere but in captivity. The feeling lasted, with diminishing intensity, sometimes for days. Always it was a tonic. It sprang, he felt, from the realization that he had no possessions, no responsibilities, no family ties or obligations about which he could do anything; he was completely absolved. Part too of the sensation was the conviction that the worst the Germans could do would be to harm his body, perhaps destroy it — that was all. The fact that he felt this 'that was all' made him wonder whether these feelings might not be the first stage in his becoming 'barbed-wire happy', but, as he never felt any urge to take the last logical step and climb the stockade fence, he thought it could not be dangerous. While the feeling lasted, he felt uplifted and strangely contemptuous of the guards with their constant petty preoccupations with insignificant discipline and their worries about home leave and foreign postings. At the same time he began to understand how easily and willingly one could throw one's life away.

Those, who have not themselves been a POW will find it extraordinary that the word 'happy' should be used in this connection, in fact, in any other context than when the POW learns that at last he is to be free, yet one finds the Bamboo Doctor referring to people becoming 'quite happy':

> 'It was at these two camps that we volunteers and many others really learned to adapt ourselves to the fact of being prisoners. We had to re-shape and re-direct our whole outlook: life became a game of make-believe and we acquired the knack of turning our attention entirely away from personal discomfort and deprivation. Together with a sense of humour this psychological technique saved morale and life as well. As a doctor I had many opportunities of studying the mental reactions of my fellow prisoners, and all too often I saw men failing to adapt themselves to this make-believe game, this mental camouflage of reality, and then in consequence becoming morose and gloomy and, in the end, invariably dying.'

Another who found mental camouflage for his reality was a German POW in Britain, Kurt Bock, who is quoted as having written:

> 'Talking to friends, talking and talking round and round. Have we ever again had time for these discussions? I certainly have not and I regret it. Everybody had his own life story and there was also the present and, even more important, the problems to come . . . There was nothing hectic about it . . . It could be compared to monastic life . . . . But I do not think this time was lost: I even think of it as a nice time.'

So speaks the eternal undergraduate.

As is understandable, some prisoners lost the will to live, and, when that happened, the person concerned was really beyond help. The Bamboo Doctor has described how they used subterfuge to keep people cheerful, inventing good news about the progress of the war. It was sometimes possible to order those who were past caring to 'get better' and, if the instinct of obedience was sufficiently strong, this occasionally worked, but usually they were doomed.

Shortage of food, the greatest enemy of the POW, as well as being an anti-aphrodisiac, the cause of beri-beri and other deficiency diseases, had another effect that is seldom mentioned: constipation. The Bamboo Doctor records how in several of the camps for which there are records, the normal period between bowel movements settled down at between ten and 12 days; though quite a number of people found that they only went every 20 days. The boundary between deficiency and sufficiency in the physical sense is remarkably narrow. One German POW who returned from Russia, marvelling at the way the spirit depends on the body, went on to say:

> 'Before, we had always believed that it was the spirit that built the body.

Here, in captivity, it became obvious how closely the two depend on each other. While a few more calories was often enough to get both going again. When do we in the West ever stop to think that a bigger man may be destroyed by a ration that a smaller man would survive on?

Yet others were not so sure and credited the spirit with greater strength than that:

'One thing I realized, that I was able to survive these hardships, not because of my iron constitution and strength, not by cheating or cunning. It proved the truth of the old saying that faith is a divine force, that all the self-discipline of my youth had not been for nothing.'

And again:

'What impressed me most was the unshakeable resoluteness of individual officers and crews, who, despite the direst physical and mental peril and the threats of the mass of the prisoners, even when hunger was at its direst, remained exemplary soldiers.'

'Here I have had to learn what hunger and cold really meant, what physical work in the most arduous circumstances was; here I have witnessed man in all his frailty and nakedness — in his need for salvation — but also in his quiet greatness.'

Such was the Western POW when pressures on him were extreme. Where camps were visited by representatives of the protecting power and of the International Red Cross, the scale of degradation and greatness, too, was considerably reduced, though the same phenomena were there to be observed. Francis Ambrière has described how some of the POWs descended to quite ignoble methods to preserve their comforts, not because that was imperative in order to survive, but because they were opportunists and not averse to currying favour with their captors.

Those who had to work (ORs and junior NCOs) and the relatively few officers who volunteered to do so — a thing permitted, though, in World War II at least until the end of hostilities felt to be somehow morally wrong — were better able to endure captivity than those who had to have recourse to lectures, classes, amateur theatricals and what today are called leisure pursuits, in a frantic endeavour to fill their time. Manual labour is a good soporific and leaves few hours of the day to be filled. Obviously some benefited by their studies, others by what they saw at work and the insights it gave. One German, a POW in World War II, has recorded with gentle irony how much he learned as a POW. He learned he said:

'how to build roads and repair streets, how to fell trees, many of the farmer's skills, how to drive mules, how to cobble and make shoes and clothes; how to launder underclothes. I learned how to make handkerchiefs out of an old sheet and foot-wrappings out of old handkerchiefs. I learned how to cook and to appreciate the worth of food. I learned a lot about human nature, as months of hunger and deprivation made people lay aside their culture and selfcontrol and become mere hungry animals. I became acquainted with unveiled envy and jealousy, cold disinterestedness towards those who possessed nothing and feline ingratiation as soon as one of them acquired anything edible or smokeable; so that often I would have preferred the honest tail-wag of a dog to their affected friendliness. I learned, too, to anticipate with stoicism the daily ups and downs that are the lot of the POW, who never knows what will happen

Forestry and agriculture absorbed a lot of POW labour in both world wars. Here, prisoners of the Austrians are unloading timber, baling hay, and doing farm work during World War I. No guards in sight.

to him the next day. I learned especially to respect one's daily bread and to believe in God's just steering of our destiny that we, poor wretches, often comprehend so little and rebel against so wildly and bitterly.'

SEX AND THE POW

One aspect of a man's mental and physical make-up that must be affected by being kept imprisoned with hundreds, even thousands of others in close, if not cramped quarters, is his sexual urge, elementary and not always easily suppressed. This problem does not seem to have been seriously discussed until after World War I, though it must always have existed. The dominant factor here is undoubtedly diet.

Eric Newby has recounted how when the girls of Fontanella used to parade provocatively on Sundays along the road that bordered their prison, the British POWs (and the Italian guards) got much pleasure out of watching them from the windows, even though a head leaned out was liable to attract a sentry's bullet. They were not, he explained, unduly troubled by the lusts of the flesh. He quoted one of his friends as saying 'It isn't that one wants to poke them. I'm not sure I could do it any more, but it would be heaven just to be with them . . .'

Robert Guerlain, a Frenchman who was in a German POW camp several hundred miles to the north, has described how they used to see some of the local maidens walking on Sunday on the arm of their uniformed escorts; many were young, some even pretty, yet they scarcely thought of them as women. They aroused no desire, awoke no memories, they were just part of the landscape beyond the barbed wire — 'the soldiers with their Sunday caps and regulation white gloves, the watch-towers with their machine-guns, the flags with the double crosses. They, too, like the rest, must be war machines.'

Eric Newby, describing his experiences, goes on:

'It was fortunate that most of us felt as he did. Had we felt otherwise, there was not much we could do about it except pull our puddings, and to perform that operation while lying cheek by jowl with twenty-six other people in a room which was illuminated by search-lights, required a degree of stealth which had deserted most of us since leaving school. Nevertheless, some of the more vigorous among us revived these ancient skills.

'Even more difficult for the residents of the *orfanotrofio* (which did duty as the POW camp) was any kind of homosexual act. Whatever loves there were between prisoners could only be expressed by looks and words, or perhaps a surreptitious pressure of the hand, otherwise they had to remain locked away within the hearts and minds of the lovers until they could be free or were moved to some more private place.'

Others had fewer inhibitions or greater opportunities, for A J Barker has quoted Jim Witte as telling how a certain corporal in the Military Police fell in love with a young soldier who played female roles in the camp theatricals, and how, at one roll call, both were missing. They were eventually found snuggled down under a blanket in a corner of another compound. The Italians — this was an Italian POW camp in World War II — were highly amused and put the two in solitary confinement together for a week. In this camp, during the winter, when rations were meagre and the supply of Red Cross parcels irregular, love 'took a back seat'; but when summer and ample rations returned 'Cupid came into his own again'. Elsewhere it is recorded that when stomachs were full masturbation was relatively common.

In Germany, in World War I as well as World War II, most of the POWs in working parties sent out daily to factories or those who lived and worked on farms were adequately fed and many ended up with a girl friend, who might be a conscripted civilian from Poland or elsewhere, or a local woman whose husband was either dead or at the front. On one farm, the four British POWs working there used to meet the Polish women workers each evening, each in a different part of the farm for the sake of privacy: the fact that none could understand the other making no difference. The four had to rush back to be locked in at the appointed hour by the elderly German soldier who was supposed to be in charge of them, but he was tolerant and often prepared to wait. Then, as Stuart Brown records: 'The nights became colder, the frosts keener, the winds more biting, killing passion difficult enough to generate when clad as thickly as we were.' Then the daughter of the farm returned from college and she fell in love with Stuart Brown and ran very considerable risks to associate with him. Happily, all went well and they eventually married, as did a number of POWs employed in agriculture in Britain (and elsewhere) in both wars.

Another British POW, who worked on a building site in World War II, has described the extent of the fraternization between the women workers and the POWs. At this building site the POWs and the male and female foreign labourers went out to work at 6 am while their German bosses did not arrive on the site until an hour later, thus providing an hour for 'fraternization'. There was a certain amount of free time at lunch, when the men could roam about the site more or less at will. In the summer they swam in the canal. At this building site, as in most factories, the girls were mostly foreigners, but there were plenty of German women on the farms and towards the end of World War II, when in Germany shortages were becoming acute, the attractions of the POWs Red Cross parcels began to prove more than many of them could resist, even though to be caught fraternizing meant having your head shaved and being sent to prison. On farms, however, where the POW had replaced the man on the farm, it was almost an accepted fact that he should assume marital as well as husbandry duties.

In Germany fraternization between German women and POWs or foreign civilian workers was strictly forbidden on grounds of Nazi ideology; in Great Britain and the USA it was similarly forbidden, but as a form of reprimand to bring home to Axis prisoners the wickedness of their government in starting the war in the first place. This ban on fraternization remained in force in the UK until July 1947, when the publicity given to the case of an ATS girl, Monica Cann, and a German POW, Leo Gunter, who married secretly because a baby was on the way, led to its being reviewed. Gunter had been court-martialled and sentenced to 12 months in prison, but after the review the sentence was remitted, as were those passed on 26 other POWs who had 'associated' with British girls.

Obviously, 27 was not the total number of such associations. Didcot Camp may or may not have been typical. One prisoner there, Eiserbeck, has described how he and three other prisoners frequently got over the wire at night and through the depot fence to freedom. They went to pubs, where they met ATS and civilian girls for a drink and a cuddle. One publican even put his own sitting-room at their disposal, making it 'for POWS only'. At one stage, the four got hold of some small tents and pitched these in a sort of No-man's Land outside the camp and in them entertained their friends.

The fact that this sexual activity could go on is proof that restricted as the rations were in Great Britain at the end of the war and after the cessation of hostilities, when huge quantities of food had to be shipped to the liberated countries of the Continent as well as to occupied Germany, the food that everybody, POWs included, had was more than enough.

On the other side of the Atlantic, it is recorded that most of the break-outs from the POW camp at Evansville, Indiana, where rations were more than ample, were not attempts to escape and get back to Germany, but made in order to get to the local brothel area.

Diet does seem to have been all important where the sexual urge is concerned. After Germany's capitulation, when liberated American POWs were being collected in centres before being sent home, the Americans sent a concert party to entertain the men in their big staging post, Camp Lucky Strike, at Le Havre. The party included a number of glamorous chorus girls but almost no one watched them. A Red Cross official, surprised at the lack of interest in girls, was told: 'Well, ma'am, they are feeding me 12 vitamin pills a day now, but before I'll be interested in women again they'll have to feed me 24.'

AN INTRIGUING FOOTNOTE

The Bamboo Doctor has described how in the camps of British POWs in Siam towards the end of the war, improved diet awakened physical urges which the ladies of Siam were happy to gratify in return for socks! At first the camp gallants generously paid with a complete pair, but they soon discovered that one sock tonight, the other tomorrow night was just as acceptable. These visits to the local ladies were, of course, illicit and had to be made under the wire and across bamboo canes spanning a 15 ft (4.5m) ditch, which the prisoners had had to dig. (This ditch was intended to be a mass grave for POWs in the event of the Allies making a successful landing in Siam or Malaysia, when all Allied POWs were to be killed. The two atom bombs on Nagasaki and Hiroshima forced Japanese capitulation before these landings were made, saving the lives of many thousands of Allied soldiers.)

There is an intriguing footnote to the question of sex and the POW, which illustrates the the Bamboo Doctor's profound knowledge of human nature. One of the rivers of Siam in which British POWs used to bathe was infested with great shoals of fish only two or three inches long, but of very vicious habit. The POWs bathed naked and the little fish tended to nibble at their private parts. Realizing that the resulting scars would be capable of misinterpretation by insurance doctors, wives or girlfriends, the Bamboo Doctor gave the victims certificates, written on any odd scrap of paper, certifying the true cause of the scars.

The other side of the coin is the effect of a man's captivity on the women he has left at home. The enforced absence and uncertainty as to how long the separation would last, inevitably led to cases of infidelity and some POWs lived in dread of receiving the postcard or letter that would tell them of their replacement by another man. The problem is as old as captivity and guidelines for dealing with it were first laid down by the Assyrians 4500 years ago. According to the Code of Hammurabi, if, when a man was taken prisoner in war, there was still food in his house, i.e. his wife and children were properly provided for, his wife could not go to another man without being punished ('thrown into the water'); but if the larder was or became empty, i.e. there was no provision for her, and she went to another man, no blame was to attach to her. When her husband returned — if he returned — she had to go back to him, but any children she may have had with the other man remained with their father.

Another course of treatment the effectiveness of which has been questioned is reeducation, also called indoctrination or brain washing. The normal POW is an apolitical animal and will agree to anything that will not injure his own side, if to do so will improve his lot. Out of the tens of thousands of American service men brainwashed by the Chinese/Koreans only 22 elected to remain in the land of their adopted philosophy.

In World War II it was considered that the German POWs had all been exposed to the moral contagion of that nasty disease, Nazism, and that the Allies ought to use their captivity to try to cure those who had caught the infection, before they were released back to their homes after having atoned to some extent for the sins of their country through manual labour for the Allies. To further this aim, a system of 'reeducation' was introduced. The reeducation system was a baby brother of brainwashing and no more effective. Indeed, it is difficult not to agree with Dr Harald Dreier, one of the British reeducation team, who is quoted as having said:

'Re-education was a very ambitious undertaking — one might even say a presumptuous scheme. In my eyes it was totally superfluous. The lectures and discussions could have made no lasting impression on POWs who were camp followers, whom the English authorities had screened as more or less harmless. Camp followers are just camp followers: yesterday of the Nazis; today of democracy; tomorrow of the Communists. For these, the course was a pleasant change from the dreariness of camp life. The anti-Nazi needed no re-education. The appeal was in the main really to the trade-union and Marxist-Communist oriented participants, who took the lead in the discussions. All that remained for the democratically-minded POWs was to exchange information and opinions in private groups during breaks. . . .'

Another commentator, Siegfried Bandelow, wrote:

'. . . it was at this point that the so-called re-education began. This was done in a very clumsy way. Very many of the speakers were unable to put themselves into the state of mind of the German officers they were dealing with. From my notes it emerges that most of the lecturers did not understand that the German POWs regarded themselves first and foremost as German officers and that political questions — National-Socialism, anti-semitism, etc. — were for them only something with which they did not or could not identify. . . .'

C H A P T E R   8

ESCAPE

Ever since soldiers have been taken prisoner, escape has been the dream of most captives, and the effect of that dream in causing them to organize secretly and actively has been the best therapy for the psychological ills of captivity.

Modern technology has enormously reduced the chances of successful escape. But before the invention of the telegraph and telephone, for example in the Napoleonic Wars, once you were well away from your place of confinement, if you had money and were not too scruffy in appearance, there was little to prevent you getting away altogether. In those days, foreign travel was general and foreigners were everywhere, even in time of war, so that neither a foreign accent nor an inability to speak the language of the country aroused suspicion. With sufficient funds and the appearance at least of a gentleman you could go anywhere more or less without question. Escaping from the actual camp was, then as now, a question of tunnelling, impersonation or climbing a wall or fence, except for those who broke parole, ie. were already living outside. These latter were obviously at a great advantage. Of the 462 French officers who broke parole between 1810–12, 307 at least reached France. One of the most blatant examples of this breaking of an officer's word was that of General Lefebre, who was on parole in Cheltenham, where he had been joined by his wife. Lefebre was a man of affluence and lived very comfortably, but even so he was irked by the few restrictions placed on his movements and decided to escape. To do this, he decided to impersonate a German count of his acquaintance and had his wife dress as a boy and pretend to be his son, while his aide-de-camp dressed and acted as his valet. The trio first went to London, where they stayed at an hotel in Jermyn Street, while the authorities prepared their travel documents. When these were ready, they took coach to Dover and from there crossed to France, from the safety of which the General later wrote an insolent letter to the British Government explaining why he had considered it his 'duty' break his word. Things have changed considerably since those days and were it not extraordinary what brazen cheek and self-assurance can achieve, one would be tempted to suggest that no Lefebre could get away with that today.

The first recorded escape of a POW is, perhaps, that of the Thracian Spartacus, who, after his capture by the Romans, had been sold to the gladiatorial school of Lentulus at Capua. He and 70 of his fellows overpowered their guards, armed themselves and took refuge on Mt Vesuvius, where they were joined by other runaway slaves. For three years they defied the Roman army's best endeavours to recapture them, often inflicting humiliating defeats on the troops sent against them. They even fought their way to the north of Italy, where there was little between them and escape from Roman-controlled territory, but 'the gods disordered their minds' and they turned south again away from the snows and the cold, and so to final defeat and death. Such an escape of gladiators, who were slaves, was a thing the Romans had always dreaded and done their best to guard against, so that the organization of the original escape must have been consummate and the element of luck, perhaps, not all that considerable.

One other who escaped by force of arms was Count Maurice Beniowski, a Pole who had been captured by the Russians near Tarnapol and was being sent with other POWs to Kazan, a protracted journey in the course of which they found themselves quartered in private houses in Tula. One night Beniowski went down in his underclothes (POWs did not have pyjamas or nightshirts in those days) to answer a knocking at the front door. The man at the door proved to be a Russian officer come with an escort to collect Beniowski. He asked if the Count was in, obviously not knowing that he was talking to the man he wanted. Beniowski replied that he was upstairs, and, as the Russians mounted the staircase, Beniowski walked out into the night and straight to the house where a fellow POW, a Swedish officer, was lodged. The two decided that this was the moment to escape. In those days before the telephone their chances were quite good. They walked briskly out of the town and at the next village 'took horses' and rode to Sebukfar, where the local (Ukrainian) gentry were in the midst of one of their periodic hate-campaigns against all things Russian, and so were delighted to help. They provided the two with an order for post horses, money and some clothing, and off they set again. At Nizhny Novgorod they pretended to be officers on their way back to Petersburg and were dined by the Woiewod who gave them a letter of recommendation to his opposite number in Volodomir, and so they progressed through Moscow, Twer and Welki Novgorod, reaching Petersburg on November 19. There they put up at an hotel, the Swedish major posing as Beniowski's valet so that they could share a room. From a German apothecary they obtained the name and address of a Dutch ship's captain who would be prepared to take them 'into another country', and arranged to pay him 500 ducats on reaching Holland. The captain, however, sold them to the Russian police and they were recaptured.

Sent to Kamchatka the Count began planning to escape along with the other disaffected exiles and prisoners, of whom there was a considerable number. He attracted the attention of the Governor of Kamchatka, and before long Beniowski found himself tutoring the Governor's three children, teaching them arithmetic, French, chess and instructing them in the social graces, while entertaining the Governor's wife and her daughters with stories of European society. The younger of the two daughters, Anastasia, fell in love with the very personable Count and, although Beniowski could not renounce the advantage of having an informant and helper in high places, he resisted her in deference to his wife at home. In the end, however, circumstances, particularly the insistence of his fellow prisoners, forced him to agree to an official betrothal. By this time Beniowski was allowed to live as a free person and had talked the Governor into agreeing to an ambitious plan to build a new settlement in the south of the peninsula, where, Beniowski assured him, it would be possible to grow corn on a considerable scale and so provide Kamchatka with a valuable addition to its commissariat. The Governor provided the 'settlers' with all the equipment they needed for this project, and even supplied them with muskets and powder so that they could hunt and pay their taxes in furs, as other Kamchatkans did.

Beniowski meanwhile continued to plan a multiple escape. When this plan was discovered, he was warned by the Governor's daughter in time to take countermeasures. These included seizing hostages, and then using his 70 men, all experienced soldiers, to capture the fort. The Governor put up a spirited resistance which ended when he was shot dead in front of his wife and daughter. There were still 700 Cossacks to be dealt with, and Beniowski forced them to lay down their arms by herding their wives and daughters into the wooden church and threatening to burn it over their heads unless they did so. The Cossacks believed that he was capable of carrying out his threat, and surrendered, leaving Beniowski in de facto control of all Kamchatka, where he could have remained and lorded it for a considerable time. Instead, he sent a contingent of his men to the mouth of the river Bolshoy, where they found a ship, the *St Peter & St Paul*, which they seized and then loaded with stores, arms and 36 barrels of vodka, plus a huge quantity of furs, which the Governor had collected in lieu of taxes and which they took in order to provide them with funds, perhaps even capital, once they were back in civilization. Taking with them the Governor's daughter Anastasia, who, although she must have held Beniowski indirectly responsible for her father's death, loved the Count so sincerely that she was prepared to throw in her lot with his, they put to sea on May 6, 1771, heading south. They were free at last.

Beniowski and his companions were all soldiers, and although they had subborned the ship's crew into working the ship for them, they were short of navigational skills, apart from which the Sea of Ochotsk, the Bering Sea and even the Sea of Japan were all but unknown to Westerners, so when they ran into dirty weather they also ran into trouble. They made landfall off one of the Japanese islands, stayed some week in a part of Formosa that was then an independent kingdom, and finally reached Maçao on September 21. Here a number of survivors — including the Governor's daughter Anastasia — died, 23 of them from overeating.

Another case of force majeure and love combining in a successful escape, was that of some Frenchmen who had landed in 1797 at Fishguard with the intention of invading England through Wales, an enterprise that was one of Napoleon's fiascos. The captured French were imprisoned near Fishguard and, like their compatriots in other prison-camps, sought to eke out their meagre subsistence allowance by making toys and knick-knacks to sell to the civilians. The bits and pieces needed for this work were brought in by two local girls employed in taking away the prison refuse. The girls fell in love with two of the Frenchmen and formed a plan to rescue them and the others in the same barracks, 100 in all. From a shin of beef the girls brought into the camp, the Frenchmen made digging tools with which they began constructing a tunnel, the two girls carrying away the soil in their buckets. When the tunnel was complete, they waited until the two girls tipped them off that a boat capable of carrying their number had put in. The first suitable vessel was a sloop with a load of anthracite for Stackpole, but when the Frenchmen had made their way through the tunnel and down to the water-side, seized the sloop and tied up the crew, they found that their craft was lying high and dry and it was impossible to get her off. Alongside the sloop was a yacht belonging to Lord Cawdor and this they managed to launch, but she could not accommodate anything approaching their number. In the end the two girls, their lovers and 23 other men went aboard, taking with them the sloop's compass, water casks and provisions. Some way out they caught up with another sloop (this one laden with corn) captured her and, abandoning the yacht, compelled the crew to sail the sloop to France where all ended happily in a double wedding.

With the invention of the telegraph and telephone, escape became much more difficult and considerably more luck was required to supplement the daring of the individual. In World War I escaping became almost a sport, with rather less than a sporting chance of success. 'I don't think there is anything I have ever done,' wrote A J Evans in *The Escaping Club*, 'quite so exciting as escaping from prison. It may not be the same for other men who have tried both fighting in the air and escaping, but I know that for me the 'nervous tension' before the latter is much greater than anything I have experienced at the front . . . In my opinion,' he went on, 'no prisoner of war has ever escaped without more than a fair share of luck, and no one ever will. However hard you try, however skilful you are, luck is an essential element in a successful escape.'

In the Napoleonic Wars an escaping officer who was recaptured not only lost his officer status, but had his rations and those of his room mates reduced to two-thirds until the saving had covered all the extra costs incurred in the hunt and recapture and in repair of tunnels, holes and any damage done.

WHEN ESCAPING IS A CRIME

In World War I the author of *The Escaping Club* records how he and those like him captured later in the war found it difficult to understand the attitude of those who had been in captivity much longer and had already suffered much. 'When I first came to the camp,' he wrote, 'escaping was looked upon almost as a crime against your fellow prisoners. One officer stated openly that he would go to considerable lengths to prevent an escape, and there were many who held he was right. There is much to be said on the side of those who took this view. Though it was childishly simple to escape from the camp, to get out of the country (Turkey) was considered next to impossible. An attempt to escape brought great hardships and even dangers to the rest of the camp, for the Turks had made a habit of strafing with horrible severity the officers of the camp from which the prisoner had escaped.' To a certain extent this went for Germany too, as punishments for trying to escape could be quite severe there, though not as severe as those inflicted by the Japanese in World War II, who beheaded any officer who had escaped and been recaptured; in some cases prisoners were organized in tens and, if one attempted to escape, the other nine were automatically executed.

The difficulty of getting away from an established place of detention is the main reason why the best time to escape is before you get to one, though as the person concerned is likely to be exhausted by the events that led to surrender, perhaps even wounded, physically he will be at a disadvantage, for to escape successfully you need to be fit. However, if you are trying to escape from enemy-occupied territory, as so many did in World War II, there is a reasonable chance that there will be a local escape organization to look after you. The realization that the best time to escape is before you are captured led to many aids to escape (compasses in buttons, maps in heels, hack-saws in shoe laces, etc) being incorporated in the uniform or equipment of those most likely to need them ie, air crews.

Realizing the advantages of early escape, some have tried to make a dash for freedom from the marching column when on the way to a camp after capture, or, especially in the case of ORs, on their way to a place of work. Attempts have met with varying success. In the Peninsular Wars (1808–14), for example, Spanish soldiers captured near Torquemata made a dash for it and managed to reach some wine caves where they hid. The French rooted them out and recaptured two, whom they shot in order to discourage the others. An English officer engaged on the other side wrote that 'Although not entirely without excuse, this act is clearly unjustifiable. If a prisoner runs away, and the guard shoots him in the act, he has done no more than he ought, because when the prisoner runs he is no longer surrendered, and is an enemy, the capture of whom is doubtful. But when he is retaken, you may put him in irons, not to punish him, but to secure him, for he has committed no crime and to kill him is murder.'

This view was adopted by Professor Francis Lieber, who had himself been a POW, having served under Blücher at Liegnitz, Waterloo and Namur, and who drafted the 'Instructions for the Government of the Armies of the United States', which led to General Order 207 of July 3, 1863 which stated:

> A prisoner of war who escapes may be shot, or otherwise killed in flight; but neither death nor any other punishment shall be inflicted on him for his attempt to escape, which the law of order does not consider a crime. Stricter means of security shall be used after an unsuccessful attempt to escape.

Jean Brilhac has described how in an occupied country, such as Poland in 1940, where the civilian population is actively sympathetic to those attempting to escape:

> 'a gesture or look is often sufficient for a Pole to risk his life on your behalf. A column of French prisoners is being led to work one early morning. Suddenly, while sentries are not looking, one of the prisoners dives into the ditch by the side of the road. He is followed by a second and by a third. No one has seen them except a peasant woman on her way to work. She is a Pole. She sees that they are French, and knows that if they remain in the open country they will find no shelter and will be recaptured. She walks back to her barn, steps inside for a moment, and then comes out again, purposely leaving the door ajar. She makes a tiny movement to the prisoners, so imperceptible that unless you were desperately on the alert you would never have noticed it. This sign means: "Don't remain in that ditch. You'll be caught and beaten to death. There's my barn: use it." Then she disappears into the field. Not a word has been spoken. The three men slip into the barn: they find that

A German ferret (as the special guards assigned to detect escapes were known in camp slang) poses in a tunnel mouth in this picture taken by the captors for their escape records. His improvised trowel is a piece of barracks floorboard and he holds a metal basin for disposing of earth.

the peasant woman has even placed a ladder under the loft, so that they can climb up and bury themselves in the warmth of the hay until nightfall. They will never see the peasant woman again. They will never be able to thank her. They don't even know her name, and probably have never seen her face.'

These three successfully made their way to London thanks to that combination of luck and bravery. There are three basic ways of getting out of a prison

Seventy-six prisoners used this tunnel (affectionately known as Harry) in the first stage of their escape from Stalag Luft 3 at Sagan on March 25, 1944. Seventy-three were recaptured and fifty of these executed. The Gestapo wanted to gaol the camp commandant for negligence.

or a prison camp; you can go under, through or over the obstacles put to keep you in, but the first step, before you attempt any of these methods, is to decide to escape. From the moment of taking the decision, you begin to feel free — long before you have tried to escape, let alone succeeded. Plenty of would-be escapers have never finished an escape, in the way, as one French writer puts it, that there are poets who have never finished a poem. Psychologically, what matters is the decision to try and the peace of mind, the occupation and the revitalization of the imagination and mind that comes with it.

'Going under' means tunnelling and this is far and away the most popular method of escape. In every age prisoners have tried it and quite a number have 'moled' their way to freedom. One who started a tunnel but was lucky enough not to use it, was Julius Lauterbach, a merchant navy captain of the Hamburg-Amerika line. As a reserve officer he was recalled in 1914 and in November of that year was serving on the notorious German cruiser, *Emden*, then in Far Eastern waters. Lauterbach was given the job of sailing a German coaling ship, *Erford*, to neutral waters, while the *Emden* tried to decoy the British ships stationed near the Cocos Islands away from her. Lauterbach thought he had done his job and sailed *Erford* into Dutch colonial (Javanese) waters, but the British navy disagreed with him and took him and his ship to Singapore, where Lauterbach was sent to a POW camp.

He determined to escape. The method he chose was tunnelling and he and several others set to work. They had made considerable progress, though they had not gone nearly far enough, when the Indian troops who guarded the camp became disgruntled because they thought the British had broken a promise to send them home by a certain date. They mutinied and killed the white officers and administrative staff in the camp, before making off, leaving the gates wide open. Lauterbach and his companions were able to walk out, taking all their belongings with them. Well supplied with money, they had no difficulty in making their way to the Dutch colony of Java, where since this was neutral territory, they were safe. Lauterbach travelled as a civilian passenger by ship to Shanghai, San Francisco, New York and Copenhagen back to Germany.

'Going through' takes various forms. The most straightforward is to bluff one's way out. This method is favoured by linguists, who have often been tempted to put their knowledge of their captors' language to good use. One who tried this was a Frenchman in Norman Cross during the Napoleonic Wars. He must have been quite handy with a needle, for he made himself a complete uniform of the Hertfordshire Militia, which was then providing the guard for the camp, and a wooden replica musket properly coloured and surmounted with a tin bayonet. One day, he donned his home-made uniform, and, when the guard was being changed, mingled with those who were going off duty. He marched out with them and into the guard room, but there his luck ran out. The others all placed their muskets in the rack provided, but the Frenchman's replica, which he had had to measure by eye, was a couple of inches too tall and would not go in. This was noticed, and the Frenchman was marched back to prison.

Another optimist was a Russian officer in Zorndorf Camp, near Cüstrin in East Prussia, during the First World War. He spoke perfect German — he had probably attended a German university — and had patiently made or collected a complete German officer's uniform; so one day, he put on his uniform and, a home-made saddle over his left arm, left hand clasping an equally makeshift bridle, he strode out past the sentries, peremptorily brushing aside any suggestion or request that he show a pass or identity card. Having got out, his intention had been to steal a decent horse from somewhere and ride back to Russia. Unfortunately an NCO who happened to be working outside the camp, had noticed that the sentries had not been shown a pass or identity card, and, being a stickler for the rules, walked across to put the matter right — and that was that.

Another method is to get yourself conveyed out in a refuse cart, laundry box or whatever conveyance is used to cart things out of the camp. The most extreme case on record is that of an unnamed Polish officer who went out sitting stark naked in the sewage cart used to empty the latrines, his clothes in a waterproof bundle on his head. Then, of course, there is the method of cutting through the wire, but this is a lengthy process prone to discovery and not often successful.

ROBERT NEBAU'S EPIC ESCAPE

Finally, there is the method of 'going over the top'. Climbing with or without a ladder and ropes, jumping or being thrown over by a human catapult. One who went over the top was Robert Neubau, who was knocked off his bicycle and captured by the French on September 16, 1914. After a spell building roads in Brittany, where they all suffered from the fanatical anti-German sentiments and behaviour of the civilian population (the

French government did not in those days quite fulfil its obligations to protect from 'violence, insults and public curiosity') and then working in a quarry, he was transferred to Rouen, where he was employed unloading coal from ships from England. Many of the boats he unloaded were Scandinavian and their crews were far from unfriendly. The Swedes especially often slipped the POWs a slice of bread and butter or some fish, though to do so was forbidden. The mate of one ship told him that there was a Swede due to sail back to Sweden in a few days. He described her emblem and funnel markings and explained where she was berthed. It seemed a hint worth taking.

A roll-call was held on the dockside at the conclusion of each day's work, making it impossible for a prisoner to be 'left behind' in the ship in which he had been working, Neubau consequently had to get out of the camp itself. The camp was secured by a double 10 ft plank fence, the intervening space being patrolled by guards with dogs. The only way out was over the two fences sometime during the night. It was then July and the nights were very light. There was supposed to be a brief period of mist each night, but Neubau discovered that the mist came down just before dawn for too short a time to be of any real assistance.

Bastille Day, July 14 1915, ended in a pitch-black night. Rain poured down and the noise of it in the chestnut trees bordering the camp was so loud as to deaden other sounds. This was Neubau's opportunity. He put on clean underclothes, wound a length of string round his waist, flung an overcoat round his shoulders and walked out to tackle the plank fence. Taking off his clogs in order to be able to climb without making a noise, he found he could still reach the top of the fence with his finger tips. Pulling himself up, he looked over the top: no sentry or guard in sight. He let his coat fall to the ground, pulled himself over and dropped down. The second fence was criss-crossed with barbed wire and in this both trouser legs caught, tearing one knee badly: but he was quickly over and down on the other side. The rain had now stopped, but the ditch was half full of water, and he could still crawl along it on hands and knees. A patrol went past without noticing him. Then he remembered that he was still wearing his soldier's cap, put it in his pocket and replaced it with a civilian sports cap he had got from a fellow prisoner in exchange for two shirts. Otherwise he was all in unobtrusive field grey. A dash across the street brought him into the shadow cast by a large tree. Between him and the harbour, there was now only a large, brightly lit goods yard that was studded with wine barrels. Making his way between these and under some waggons he reached the quay and one of the coal ships. It was half-past ten.

The ship was Swedish with a yellow-and-blue flag painted on both sides. Neubau went aboard, knocked on the door of a cabin which had light showing in its window and walked in. Speaking German, he made his position understood to a surprised Swede, who proved sympathetic. Neubau learned that the boat he needed was on the other side of the harbour. He made swimming gestures, but the Swede shook his head and pointed to a small boat, tied up on the far side of the coal ship. Had he stopped to think Neubau would have realized, as he did when it was too late, that to leave the boat tied up on the far side of the harbour would give his pursuers a good clue to where to look for him. Reaching the other side, he stripped, put his clothes in a lighter alongside a large steamer and paddled back to the steamer from which he had taken the small boat. Having restored the boat to its place, he started to swim back, only to discover that the tide had meanwhile

This Russian POW was shot dead in the act of salvaging a cigarette tossed to him by an American POW on the other side of the wire.

turned and there was quite a strong current against him, which carried him several hundred yards below the lighter in which his clothes were. A dangling rope enabled him to climb aboard a steamer and from it reach the quay. Stark naked, but so sunburned that he was nearly invisible, especially when in shadow, he finally reached the steamer to which the lighter with his clothes was tied. He walked aboard into the arms of the nightwatchman, but again Neubau was in luck, for when the man heard 'German prisoner', he allowed Neubau to recover his clothes. He also told Neubau that neutral ships were often searched at sea and if found carrying contraband (or escaping POWs) could be sequestrated, so no one would dare to let Neubau sail with them if they knew he was aboard. He should, he was told, get aboard a ship as a stowaway.

Day was breaking as he left the ship, which was bound for England, in search of somewhere to hide. He jumped onto the deck of another steamer, dived down a companionway and found himself in the crews' quarters. A light was burning, but everyone was sound asleep. There was a trapdoor as his nightwatchman friend had described. He descended into an anchor locker which was two paces in either direction and filled with enormous iron links. There was one patch of light coming through the hawse-hole: this acted as his clock. When it began to disappear, he knew it must be evening, and when it had gone, it was obviously night. He tried to raise the trap-door but found that he could not move it. He gave a tremendous heave and the trap-door flew open with a clatter, upsetting a bucket of water that had been standing on it. Despite the clatter none of the sleepers woke up and he left the ship unnoticed.

There were a lot of people about, but by keeping in the shadows of railway waggons, he walked along unhindered until he came to a footbridge too low for a steamer to pass and realized that the ship he wanted must lie even further off on the far side of the basin. As he hesitated he noticed that the ship beside him was Swedish. A nightwatchman appeared out of the darkness and to his horror Neubau discovered that he was not a Swede but English. However, he proved also to be a pacifist and conscientous objector serving only in neutral ships and gave Neubau a first-class meal, but he could not do more, for this ship, too, was sailing for England that morning. Neubau had to leave. Taking advantage of a slowly moving goods train Neubau slipped past a group of sentries to the very ship he wanted.

Fearing that she might be searched before she sailed, he decided not to board her until the last moment. It was then 3 am on Friday and the ship was not due to sail until 6 pm the following day. Everywhere between the rails were heaps of goods covered with tarpaulins. He dived under one tarpaulin and found a pyramid of bales of waste-paper, one step of which provided a comfortable couch. There he spent the next 31 hours sleeping, dozing and listening to the noises of the port. Late on the Saturday afternoon he emerged and took up position under a railway waggon from where he could watch the ship. When he judged the time had come to try to get aboard, he emerged, jumped onto the stern deck, but caught his foot on a chain and the clatter alerted the nightwatchman. Again Neubau was lucky enough to find a sympathetic man to whom he explained his position; the nightwatchman, however, was adamant: it was too risky to let him stay aboard.

There was another ship, also bound for Sweden, lying downstream. As Neubau walked off he suddenly realized that his tread was noiseless, because he was still barefoot. Afraid that this might arouse suspicions, he decided to whistle, but the only tune he could think of was *Deutschland, Deutschland über Alles*, so off he went whistling the enemy's national anthem.

So far he had had phenomenal luck, but suddenly his mood changed. A fit of depression came over him and he told himself that he was not going to make it. He almost decided to give up trying, but coming to another neutral ship he walked aboard her as though he owned her or at least had a paid-up passenger's ticket in his pocket. No nightwatchman! No one! He walked into the galley.

At the table sat the nightwatchman, head on the table, an empty schnapps bottle beside him. Neubau managed to rouse the man sufficiently to be told that the ship had been unloaded and was sailing back to England in the morning. Neubau decided to risk going to England in the hope of there being able to jump a ship bound for a neutral country, so he let the nightwatchman go back to sleep and settled himself in the anchor-locker.

After a few hours he heard the sounds of impending departure; then the trap-door was raised and two seamen descended. One had a candle, the other carried two hooks. The cable-locker was far too small for him to escape being seen. He explained in a few words and pleadingly put his finger to his lips. The two replied with the same gesture. One corner of the locker was divided off with planking and the sailors gestured to him to get into this tiny compartment. With a tremendous roar, the anchor chain was wound in and stowed by the two men using their hooks. The two were Swedes with almost no English. When Neubau asked them the ship's destination they answered 'England and Svery', which he took to be an English port. Then the trap-door closed over his head and plunged him into darkness. Soon afterwards he heard the thump of the engines and finally the swish of water round the bows. After a while the engines suddenly stopped: were they being boarded to be searched or merely dropping the pilot? The engines started up again and Neubau heaved a great sigh of relief, curled up and went to sleep. Next morning the trap-door was raised above his head and a hand passed down a mug of coffee and a plate of bread and butter. This was repeated at dinner-time, in the afternoon and again at supper-time, when he was also handed a small pipe, some tobacco and, finally, a straw mattress. So it went on.

On the afternoon of the third day, the engines stopped again. They had arrived — but in England. The ship tied up alongside a jetty and the derricks started working. After a while the engines started up again. Was the ship moving her berth? Neubau's benefactors brought him more coffee and explained that the ship was at sea — and on her way to Sweden (Sverige, Svery). Few have had Neubau's luck.

WORLD WAR I'S CHEEKIEST ESCAPE?

One of the cheekiest escapes of World War I was that of Charles Collet, a senior NCO of France's 119th Infantry Regiment. Having escaped and been recaptured three times Charles Collet was awaiting a parcel from home which should have contained maps for a fourth attempt, when he was told that he was being transferred to another, stricter camp. Fearing that his parcel might not catch up with him and also that the new camp might be more difficult to escape from than the one he was in, he decided to stage an escape and lie low until the vital parcel arrived. He was given permission to leave the punishment cell and to go under escort to his own hut to get some personal belongings. There, while his friends conversed with the escort and used their bodies to screen Charles Collet from view, the latter dived through the window of the hut and ran to the latrines, where there was a loose plank that gave access to an unsalubrious cupboard in which various unsavoury brushes and pails were kept. He squeezed into this and there hid from 11.30 am until nightfall. Two friends got him food, which he ate in a store-hut. He then transferred to the space under the floor of one of the huts (which were raised off the ground) and made himself a comfortable nest with palliasses and blankets from the store. There he stayed for a whole week, emerging after it was dark to see his friends and collect the food they provided. Then the weather changed and it became bitterly cold, so that he had to move from under his floor to the roof space of the hut, where it was considerably warmer. Fifteen days after his 'escape', he learned that his parcel had at last arrived. It contained two maps, a compass, and (in a piece of goose quill stuck inside a cigarette) detailed information about the frontier. His friends purloined a false moustache from the camp theatre's wardrobe and he was ready to make his fourth bid for freedom.

A fatigue party of prisoners went every day to their station to collect parcels and mail and this party Charles Collet joined the next day. He worked with them in the store until the time came for them to disperse to their huts, when he hid and let himself be locked in the store. That night he got out through a trap-door and climbed the perimeter fence, three weeks after he had officially 'escaped' from the camp. This, his fourth attempt, was successful.

In World War II it was still possible to live as an 'extra' in a POW camp. Jim White was caught in the act with a German girl at the building site. where they both worked. (A German witness saw them go into a wash-house and watched through the key-hole, giving the court a vivid description of what he saw). He was tried before a civil court and sentenced to four years in jail. The night before he was due to be sent to the jail, he was spirited out of the camp cells and back to his block, where he lived underground undetected, while the Germans searched for him all over the country.

Supervision of interned soldiers could be just as strict as those of actual POWs. No neutral state can afford to be accused of breaking its neutrality and so risk hostile measures against it. One who escaped from internment (in Holland, during World War I) was a French captain called Coutisson. He was fortunate in being able to enlist the help of compatriots living nearby, who kept him hidden until the search for him had been called off and he could be put aboard a fishing-boat. The best part of his story is that of the efforts made to trace him, which even involved a gunboat.

A fellow prisoner Lieutenant Chauvin later sent Coutisson a description of what happened:

> 'Your flight was discovered at half-past nine. The lamp keeper, going into your room and seeing a motionless body, thought you were dead. He took fright and called the sentry; and the two of them, respectfully raising the sheets that covered the remains of the late captain, discovered the formerly bald pate of your helmet now covered with an abundant crop of black hair! Five minutes later the alarm was given, the port was closed, and every pair of field-glasses in the garrison raked the horizon anxiously.
>
> As luck would have it, the motor-yacht that we both noticed the night before with the two artists on board had weighed anchor early that morning. There could be no doubt that they had taken you off, and the gunboat (on guard duty off the island) was immediately sent after them to bring them back. The yacht had already reached Kampen, when to the astonishment of the passengers, the gunboat came alongside and declared her a prisoner. A prize crew, composed of the quarter-master of the gunboat and his revolver, boarded her. And two hours later the

whole of Urk crowded on to the piers and quays to see the two vessels come back, and to be present at the finding of the fugitive, who was certainly hidden in a drawer in the cabin. The unfortunate artists were unable to leave again before the next day.

'That night the gunboat, which had certainly not voyaged so much in the whole of its previous life, went back to Kampen, this time to fetch a police-dog, its master and a detective. It was unspeakably funny. The whole of Urk was on its toes. They shoved the dog's nose into your tunic, and the funeral procession began. First came the police clearing the way, then the dog, attached to a long leash; then the family, in the shape of the authorities, fuming with rage; and after them came a crowd of inhabitants, headed by a soldier carrying your tunic, as a general's tunic is borne before his coffin.

'Slowly the procession advanced, with measured tread. Suddenly, a great commotion! The police-dog disappeared into a house. The fugitive must be there! Alas! It was an unfortunate cat that the dog brought out in its mouth, and from which it was only separated with the greatest difficulty. During the two hours Fido promenaded thus through the village, searching in the most extraordinary places, in which you had certainly never set foot. Finally he sat down and meditated for a long time at the foot of the lighthouse; and then, thoroughly fed-up with the whole business, he was taken away and went to bed.'

Whatever method is used to get out of a prison camp, the best country from which to escape is an occupied one, especially where there is an efficient and widespread Scarlet Pimpernel organization for smuggling people out of the country, similar to that which existed in Denmark, Holland, Belgium, and Poland in World War II for getting airmen who had been shot down but not captured, back to England. Jean Brilhac has described the position in Poland:

'When one of our (escaping) prisoners arrived in Poland, he would be amazed to find himself suddenly protected by a powerful secret organization, which it was impossible to track down, which functioned everywhere and was obeyed by everyone. He would be immediately provided with money and civilian clothes. Strange guides would lead him to Warsaw by train. There he would spend a couple of weeks, his only orders being to change addresses every two days and not to ask his host's real name. His host would bring him clandestine newspapers and translate them to him . . . After he had spent a fortnight in hiding, he would find that this journey to Russia had been entirely organized for him, the route mapped out and a relay of guides chosen to escort him. He would cross the frontier without knowing whom to thank. One prisoner who crossed Poland from one end to the other, arrived in a town on a bicycle. A complete stranger beckoned to him and took him to his house. "Have you got a bicycle permit?" he asked. "Why isn't your mudguard painted white?" [A regulation in force at the time.] The escaped prisoner told his story. Although he couldn't give him a bicycle permit, the man immediately produced a pot of white paint and painted his mudguard. Then he told the prisoner how to cross the river. He must avoid the bridges as they were all guarded, but he should follow the towpath upstream, and after four miles he would find someone to ferry him across, the signal would be the caw of a crow . . .'

Such superb organization of course, did much to eliminate the element of luck vital to the prisoner on his own escaping through an enemy country. According to Eric Newby, Italy was the most difficult country to escape from in Europe. To quote from his *Love and War in the Apeninnes*:

'It was very difficult to get out of a prison camp in Italy. Italian soldiers might be figures of fun to us, but some of them were extraordinarily observant and very suspicious and far better at guarding prisoners than the Germans were. It was also very difficult to travel in Italy, if you did get out. The Italians are fascinated by minutiae of dress and the behaviour of their fellow men, perhaps to a greater degree than almost any other race in Europe, and the ingenious subterfuges and disguises which escaping prisoners of war habitually resorted to and which were often enough to take in the Germans: the documents, train tickets and ration cards, lovingly fabricated by the camp's staff of expert forgers; the suits made from dyed blankets; the desert boots cut down to look like shoes and the carefully bleached army shirts were hardly ever sufficiently genuine-looking to fool even the most myopic Italian ticket collector and get the owner past the barrier, let alone survive the scrutiny of the occupants of a compartment on an Italian train. The kind of going over to which an escaping Anglo-Saxon was subjected by other travellers was usually enough to finish him off unless he was a professional actor or spoke fluent Italian.'

Indeed, everywhere an escaped POW is easier to spot than a murderer whose picture is displayed on every public building. His clothes are either the remains of his uniform or civilian clothes that probably neither fit nor match. He probably does not know the language or knows so little that he gives himself away. Whether from fear or a sense of duty, the civilian population will very likely not help him, and will raise the alarm and call the police. If he travels by day, he is on edge and on watch the whole time: a barking dog demands a detour, the sight of a passer-by makes him fling himself to the ground. To avoid this, it is necessary to walk by night with all the difficulties that involves. Cold, too, is a terrible handicap from November to March. Then, when he considers that he is almost at the frontier, the escaper still has to find the actual frontier line and discover how it is guarded. Sometimes there is barbed wire to deal with, sometimes, as often in Eastern Europe, nothing to tell him when he has crossed the frontier.

The author of *The Escaping Club* once told Clayton Hutton that the escaper's worst enemy was hunger. A starving man becomes reckless: he will go too near farms and so set the dogs barking. He exposes himself in fields, as he hunts for something to eat; and he begins to make all sorts of mistakes: changing plans, crossing roads in daylight, venturing into villages, stealing, using violence, even throwing himself on the mercy of civilians. The successful escaper had to have enough energy-giving food to be independent of other sources, for the majority of failures can be attributed to lack of food. A certain amount of concentrated foodstuffs was included in the escaping equipment, secreted in the uniforms of air crews to help them escape before capture if they were shot down. It was also the reason why the Escaping Committees in officers' camps went to considerable lengths to see that all who attempted to escape did so with at least enough food — mainly from other people's Red Cross parcels — to sustain them for a few days.

As by World War II it had been accepted that it was the implicit 'duty' of all officers to try to escape, the Escape Committee became a recognizable institution in all POW camps of any size. The bigger the camp, the more essential the Committee, which gathered and stored escape lore, local information, specimens of passes, permits and all sorts of other documents from which to forge others for the use of escapers. The Committee would also help to provide compasses, maps, food, money and anything else an escaper might need. The Committee's main duty, of course, was to coordinate escapes and vet the various schemes hatched in people's minds. Each scheme had to be passed by the camp Committee, which might veto it or postpone it, if its implementation might endanger other projects. Obviously such decisions are best taken by a committee, rather than by an individual, as no one person should be asked to assume responsibility for the frustration, heartache and bitterness these decisions sometimes engender. The committees had the blessing of the Camp's Senior Officer, though he had to be kept in partial or complete ignorance of what went on, as, otherwise, he could not have dealt convincingly with the Camp Commandant.

COSMOPOLITAN COLDITZ

In some camps the prisoners were of several nationalities: in Colditz, for for example, there were Poles, British, French, Dutch, Belgians and Americans. Each nationality had its own little escape organization, if not an escape committee, each working in secret. In such conditions a certain degree of liaison between the groups became essential, since it was soon discovered that some good escape attempts failed due to lack of prior consultation. Although the nations involved were allies, the conditions of defeat and imprisonment vitiated any attempt to form an Allied Command for escapes. Human nature being what it is, defeat and humiliation generated suspicion and introversion, and made cooperation and mutual assistance (between nationalities) hollow-sounding words. Nonetheless there had to be some coordination and this was best done by an individual, who thus became a sort of 'Escape Officer'. One man can make friends with the like-minded where a Committee cannot, and one man can be more easily trusted than a group. By charm, diplomacy, and practical knowledge about escape, the Escape Officer achieved a position of some authority.

Whole books have been written on the subject of how escape equipment was sent into camps. It has been concealed in anything from a bootlace to a gramophone record (though never in a Red Cross parcel) These tricks are now so well documented that they can never be used again, and one wonders how future POWs will escape.

Of the 8000 British officers who tried to escape from Germany in World War I only some 40 or 50 succeeded in regaining their freedom before the Armistice. In World War II, there were two million French POWs in prison-camps, mainly in Eastern Germany and occupied Poland, before Russia entered the war, and of these only 186 reached the Free French in England via neutral Russia, and of these only 13 had come from central Germany.

Prisoners will always try to escape, but in the next war, if there is one, it will become much more important to see that they do not, Are we, perhaps, entering upon an era when quarter will not be given or surrender accepted?

Except for those besieged in a Kut, Warsaw or Stalingrad, surrender or capture happens quickly; yet when an armistice is signed or the enemy capitulates and the bullets cease to fly, the return to freedom is seldom anything like as speedy. Now that nations sit in moral judgment on one another and expect partial reparation from the labour of captured enemy soldiers, the POW may well find that for months, even years, he has to

Overleaf: A variety of different reactions to deliverance are discernible in this picture of Argentine POW's disembarking.

become a prisoner of peace so that by labouring for his erstwhile enemy he may atone for the sins of his former leaders. You may go off to war with a flourish of trumpets, but you cannot return to peace with anything like the same dash.

News that the war has ended, that 'all is over' apart from the difficult business of getting home — has come in many ways. Colonel Lake, in his gentleman's quarters outside Moscow, heard of the end of the Crimean War in 1856 thus:

> 'On the morning of the 30th the Governor of the place sent for me, and told me that he had just received orders to inform us that we were no longer prisoners of war, and that we might proceed home by any route we liked.'

For Ian Scott and his companions in Burma during World War II it was like this:

> 'Here it is! What we've been waiting for all along. The end of hostilities.
> We were paraded by the Bugler today at 12 noon, by the first British bugle-call we have heard for years. FALL IN! and we were on parade in a rush. Our British Camp Commandant told us the wonderful news — that a truce had been signed on 14th August. Since yesterday morning (16) we have been expecting something like this, but had not had it confirmed, and, as so many times we have had rumours that the war was over or nearly so, we had to wait before we could believe it was correct. What a wonderful feeling! Of course, we were told that for the next few days we would have to cooperate with our Commandant and behave — to make things easier for him, as the Nips are still to patrol our fences (bamboo — as they always have been) along with our own fellows forming a police force to maintain law and order. That is until our own troops from outside arrive to take charge. What a wonderful thought! We still cannot believe that it is over and our 'nightmare', our 'slough of despond', our 'Gethsemane', is at an end. God be praised! It's wonderful! My thoughts were: 'Jove, it's great! It'll not be long until I can see and be with Joan again'. I gave praise to God that he had helped and brought me through.'

One of the most moving pictures is that General MacArthur gives of the arrival of General Wainwright in 1945:

> 'Prisoners had been dribbling out of the Japanese camps almost as soon as the landings in Japan were made, and among the first of those liberated were General Wainwright and General A G Percival. They had been held in Mukden in Manchuria and had been flown back to Manila. I immediately directed that they be brought to Japan for the surrender ceremonies on the *Missouri*. I was just sitting down to dinner when my aide brought word that they had arrived. I rose and started for the lobby, but before I could reach it, the door swung open and there was Wainwright. He was haggard and aged. His uniform hung in folds on his fleshless form. He walked with difficulty and with the help of a cane. His eyes were sunken and there were pits in his cheeks. His hair was snow white and his skin looked like old shoe leather. He made a brave effort to smile as I took him in my arms, but when he tried to talk his voice wouldn't come.'

Let us hope that no such scenes will ever be enacted again.

B I B L I O G R A P H Y

Ambrière Francis *The Exiled*, 1951

Anthe, Otto *Rund um die Erde zur Front*

Ayling, E *The Second World War Experiences of (unpublished MS)*

Bailey, Ronald H *Prisoners of War — World War II*

Bardin, General *Dictionnaire Militaire*

Barker, A J *Behind Barbed Wire*,

Bellamy, Reginald Thomas *Unpublished Journal*

Benyowsky, Count Mauritius Augustus De *Memoirs and Travels of*, 1790

Best, Geoffrey *Humanity in Warfare*

Bilderman, Albert D *March to Calumny*

Böhme, Kurt W *Die deutschen Kriegsgefangenen in sowietischer Hand*

Booth, Major E *Unpublished journal*

Boothby, Charles *A Prisoner of France*, 1898

Bradbury, William C *Mass Behaviour in Battle and Captivity*, 1968

Braddon, Russell *The Naked Island*, 1952

Brilhac, Jean *The Road to Liberty*, 1945

Brown, John *In Durance Vile*, 1981

Brown, Stuart *Forbidden Paths*, 1978

Cambray, P G and Briggs, G G B *Red Cross and St. John The Official Record of the Humanitarian Services of the War Organization of the British Red Cross Society and Order of St John of Jerusalem 1939-1947*

Cartellieri, Dr *Hilfsplatz D.7.*, 1936

Colonie, M de la *The Chronicles of an old Campaigner (1692-1717)*

Corvisier, André *La Captivité militaire au XVLLme siècle*

Czapski, Józef *Na Nieludzkiej Ziemi*, 1949

Daly, Lieutenant-Colonel J K *Thirty Thousand Prisoners of War over the Beach; Military Review*, Vol 25, No 1

Datner, Szymon: *Crimes against POWs*, Warsaw, 1964

Delaville Le Roulx, J *La France en Orient au XIVe siècle*, 1886

Dlugosz, Jan *Roczniki czyli Kroniki slawnego Knólestwa Polskiego*

Ducrey, Pierre *Le Traitement des Prisonniers de Guerre dans la Gréce antique*

Edmonds, J E and Oppenheim, L *Land Warfare*

Edwards, Chilperic *The World's Earliest Laws*

Evans, A J *The Escaping Club*

Farrago, *War of Wits, Intelligence is for Commanders*

Fleischhacker, Hedwig *Die deutschen Kriegsgefangenen in der Sowietunion; Der Faktor Hunger*, 1965

Garrett, Richard *P.O.W.* 1981

Geschichte der deutschen Kriegsgefangenen des zweiten Weltkrieges

Grinnell-Milne, Duncan *An Escaper's Log*

Gross *Military Antiquities*

Guerlain, Robert *A Prisoner in Germany*, 1944

Haintz, Otto *König Karl XII von Schweden*

Halley, David *We missed the Boat*

Hetzel *Humanisierung des Krieges*

Hutton, Major G *Official Secret*

International Law Association Draft Proposals, 1921

Jones, Ewart C *Germans under my Bed*

Kinkhead, Eugene *Why they collaborated*

Kinne *The Wooden Boxes*

Kochan, Miriam *Prisoners of England*, 1980

Kriegsgebrauch in Landkrieg. Einzelheft des Grossen General-stabs Heft 31.

Lake, Colonel Atwell *Kars and our Captivity in Russia*, 1856

Laveran, A *De la mortalité des armées en campagne au point de vue de l'etiologie Annales de hygiene publique et de medecine legale* p 219, 1863

Mac Arthur, Douglas *Reminiscences*

Mansell, John W M *The Mansell Diaries*, 1977 (Private)

Manuel d'Oxford 1880 *Institute of International Law*

Meuer, C *Völkerrecht des Weltkrieges*

Miller, Charles *Battle for the Bundu*

Miller, Richard J *The Law of War*

Neubau, Robert *Kriegsgefangenen über England entflohen.*

Newby, Eric *Love and War in the Apennines*

Nicolas *A History of the Battle of Agincourt*

Official History of the Russo-Japanese War, Parts III and V

Oppenheim, L *International Law*

Pavillard, Stanley S *Bamboo Doctor*

Polybius *The Histories of, Translated by Evelyn Schuckburgh from the text of F Hultsch*

Putnam, George H *A Prisoner of War in Virginia (1864-5)*

Regulska, Halina *Dziennik z oblezonej Warszawy*, Warsaw 1982

Reitlinger, Gerald *Ein Haus auf Sand gebaut*, 1963

Runciman, Steven *A History of the Crusades*

Scheidl, Dr Franz *Die Kriegsgefangenschaft von den ältesten Zeiten bis zur Gegenwart*

Scott, Ian *Unpublished journal*

Slim, Field Marshall the Viscount *Defeat*

Into Victory

Sörensson, Per *Svenska Fångar i Ryssland 1700–1709*

Standing orders for forces on duty over POWs, W.O., pp 26–34

Statutes And Ordenances Made By Henry V At Treaty And Counseill Of Maunt

Stewart, Sidney *Give us this Day*, 1956

Streit, Christian *Keine Kameraden — Die Wehrmacht und die Sowietischen Kriegsgefanfangenen, 1941–45*

Stroh, Major General D A *Guarding Prisoners of War in Germany, Military Review*, Vol 26 No 7

Stroh, Major General D A *Technique and Procedure adopted by the 106th Division in Guarding Prisoners of War, Military Review*, Vol 26, No 7

Sullivan, Matthew Barry *Thresholds of Peace*, 1979

Thomson, Basil *The Story of Dartmoor Prison*, 1907

Thucydides *Histories*

Toothill, Captain H B *Burma Diary (unpublished)*

UN Command 57th Report for Nov 1–5, 28 US Dept State Bulletin 690.

Urlanis, Boris Zesarewitsch *Bilanz der Kriege*, 1965 *28 US Dept State Bulletin 690* (1953)

Vasey, George *Illustrations of Eating*

Walker, Thomas James, M D *The Depot for Prisoners of War at Norman Cross in Huntingdonshire*, 1796–1816

Williams, Elvet *Arbeitskommando*, 1975

INDEX

Picture Credits

MARS 1, 54, 60–61, 70, 98–99, 106–107
Victoria & Albert Museum 2–3
Imperial War Museum 17, 39, 44–45, 56, 58, 64–65,
69, 98, 102, 109, 110–111, 112–113, 116, 119,
130–131, 133, 139, 142–143, 160, 169
British Museum 18, 42, 53, 74
Edward Reeves 100–101
Keystone 32–33
Maurice Michael 2–3, 18, 21, 26, 36, 50–51, 55, 57,
63, 75, 77, 103, 117, 135, 151, 158, 175, 176, 179
Robert Hunt Library 4–5
Express Newspapers 6–7, 186–187
Sava Boyadjiev 15
Heeresgeschichllichen Museum, Vienna 26, 36, 57,
75, 87, 103, 117, 141, 148, 164
Illustration by kind permission of Falcon Press, from
For You The War Is Over 130, 155